英美文学导论

主　编　晏玉屏

副主编　姜泽卫　楚承华

中国水利水电出版社
www.waterpub.com.cn
·北京·

内 容 提 要

《英美文学导论》以英美文学中常见的小说、诗歌和戏剧三大体裁为主，围绕三大体裁的文学要素和文体特点，选取英国、美国具有代表性的作家和作品，结合相关的文学要素对文本进行分析。每个章节的构成情况如下：文学体裁介绍，体裁要素简介，代表作家及文学作品简介，作品选读以及对文本蕴含的思政主题分析。英美文学属于人文教育，是强调知识传授、能力培养与人格塑造相结合的全人教育，涵盖了文化、政治、历史、哲学等领域的知识。本教材既强调学生对于文学体裁、文学要素、代表作家及作品选读方面的学习，也积极引导学生关注文学作品中蕴含的思政元素，从而达到传递文学知识、塑造价值和提升英语思辨能力的目的。

本书适合大学英语专业本科阶段的学习者以及热爱英美文学的社会人士。

图书在版编目（ＣＩＰ）数据

英美文学导论 / 晏玉屏主编. -- 北京 ： 中国水利
水电出版社，2023.12（2024.11重印）
ISBN 978-7-5226-1973-6

Ⅰ．①英… Ⅱ．①晏… Ⅲ．①英语－高等学校－教材
②英国文学－文学研究③文学研究－美国 Ⅳ．
①H319.39

中国国家版本馆CIP数据核字(2023)第243214号

策划编辑：陈艳蕊　　　责任编辑：邓建梅　　　封面设计：苏　敏

书　　　名	英美文学导论 YING-MEI WENXUE DAOLUN
作　　　者	主　编　晏玉屏 副主编　姜泽卫　楚承华
出 版 发 行	中国水利水电出版社 （北京市海淀区玉渊潭南路 1 号 D 座　　100038） 网址：www.waterpub.com.cn E-mail：mchannel@263.net（答疑） 　　　　sales@mwr.gov.cn 电话：（010）68545888（营销中心）、82562819（组稿）
经　　　售	北京科水图书销售有限公司 电话：（010）68545874、63202643 全国各地新华书店和相关出版物销售网点
排　　　版	北京万水电子信息有限公司
印　　　刷	三河市德贤弘印务有限公司
规　　　格	170mm×240mm　　16 开本　　11.75 印张　　243 千字
版　　　次	2023 年 12 月第 1 版　　2024 年 11 月第 2 次印刷
定　　　价	58.00 元

前　言

自近代以来，中国外语教育就注重培养能读"西书"、译"西学"的人才，以探索抵御列强之道；在革命战争时期，注重培养军事翻译人才，服务对敌斗争之需；新中国成立后，培养多语种外交外事人才成为打开我国对外工作新局面的钥匙；改革开放后，中国外语教育为经济建设、对外交往和社会发展铺路架桥；新世纪急需高素质复合型外语人才以服务国家全球发展和海外合作。历史充分证明，外语教育只有与时俱进，才能服务时代之需，发出时代之声，回应时代之问，培养时代新人。

新时代中国高等外语教学对于传播中国文化，讲好中国故事，服务国家对外战略起到了重要作用。外语类课程的教学内容是哲学、历史、文化、文学等各种思想的汇聚地，外语课程教学过程中的思想教育的隐性功用不容忽视。2016 年，习近平总书记在全国高校思想政治工作会议上强调，"要坚持把立德树人作为中心环节，把思想政治工作贯穿教育教学全过程，实现全程育人、全方位育人、努力开创我国高等教育事业发展新局面。" 2020 年 5 月，教育部印发了《高等学校课程思政建设指导纲要》（以下简称《纲要》）。《纲要》指出，要在所有高校、所有学科专业全面推进课程思政建设，发挥每门课程的思政教育作用，提升高校人才培养质量。在培养新时代国际人才的大背景下，外语学习是实现中外沟通的桥梁，也是开展高校课程思政改革的主要阵营之一。

文学是对世界的形象化、典型化的描述，充满感性地凝结着一个民族的风土人情、价值观念、伦理道德。英美文学课程属于人文教育，强调知识传授、能力培养与人格塑造相结合的全人教育。根据《普通高等学校本科外国语言文学类专业教学质量国家标准》，外语类专业知识中的文学内涵既包括语言对象国文学，也涉及涵盖中国文学的世界文学与批评理论知识。具体指不同时期国别文学史涉及的主要作家作品，以及文学观念运动、流派和艺术成就等，并在共时层面与世界文学关联起来，以拓宽学生的外国文学视野。因此，在外国文学教学中，要将价值塑造、知识传授和能力培养融为一体，帮助学生从跨文化的视角，在读文学经典的同时，理解本国文化，更好地向世界介绍中国。

英美文学课程由于其通识性、宽博性、审美性的特点，在介绍英美文学知识和英美文学发展历史的同时，还要积极响应国家对外文化交流以及世界文明互鉴的号召。传统的英美文学课程主要包括英、美两国的文学发展史、重要文学流派、哲学思想、宗教、文化习俗、价值观等，属于西方重要代表思想的汇聚地。各类文学体裁诞生的最初原因都是服务于当时的统治阶级。比如，英国小说诞生于18世纪，当时新兴的资产阶级为了颂扬自身的资本积累、海外扩张等艰辛的创业发家史，开创了一种新的适合广大中产阶级阅读的文学体裁——小说，如笛福的《鲁滨逊漂流记》。《鲁滨逊漂流记》被视为第一部真正意义上的现代英语小说。它对当时的殖民扩张、掠夺性的原始资本积累予以肯定，具有浓厚的资本主义色彩。主人公鲁滨逊被刻画成荒岛求生的英雄，但从殖民主义视角来看，鲁滨逊就是英国早期海外殖民者的化身。为了生存，他宰杀哺育期的母羊，体现出他恃强凌弱的本性；他从食人族手中救走"星期五"并将他视为自己的仆人，体现了他内心的种族偏见和殖民压迫的思想。

因此，在鉴赏西方文学作品之美的同时，学习者也容易受到部分作品中的个人主义、利己主义以及功利主义等思想的影响，尤其是对正处于三观塑造期的大学生而言，某些思想会给他们的成长带来负面影响，此时教师的引导就显得极为重要。传统的英美文学类教材往往注重文学知识的传递，却忽视了其隐性的思想价值元素。本书在传递知识的同时不忘挖掘文字作品中的思想元素，引导学生树立正确的人生观、价值观。

《英美文学导论》以英美文学中常见的小说、诗歌和戏剧三大体裁为主，围绕三大体裁的文学要素和文体特点，选取英国、美国代表性的作家和作品，结合相关的文学要素对文本进行分析。每个章节的构成情况如下：文学体裁介绍，体裁要素简介，代表作家及文学作品简介，作品选读以及对文本蕴含的思政主题分析。英美文学属于人文教育，强调知识传授、能力培养与人格塑造相结合的全人教育，英美文学涵盖了文化、政治、历史、哲学等领域的知识。本书既强调学生对于文学体裁、文学要素、代表性作家及作品选读方面的学习，也积极鼓励学生挖掘文学作品中蕴含的思想元素，并给予正确的引导，从而达到传递文学知识、塑造价值和提升英语思辨能力的目的。

本书有以下三个特点：一、打破传统文学类书籍以历史脉络阐释文学发展的局限，本书按照文学体裁分章节进行文学知识点的梳理；二、不拘泥于作家作品的简单介绍，本书按照文学体裁的要素赏析文学作品；三、本书关注文学作品背后隐性的德育功能，注重挖掘作品中的思政要素，启发学生对相关问题的思考，发挥文学教学立德树人的功用。

本书的具体章节内容如下：

第一章绪论：介绍文学的定义、文学的常见体裁，阐释文学教学与思政教育之间的关系。

第二章小说：介绍小说的起源，讨论小说的几大要素（故事和情节、背景和主题、人物和人物塑造、叙事者和叙事视角），选读并赏析代表性的作家作品，如康拉德、毛姆、梅尔维尔、沃克等，浅析选读作品蕴含的思政主题。

第三章诗歌：介绍诗歌的起源及诗歌的种类，讨论诗歌的要素（韵律与节奏、诗歌中的修辞等），选读并赏析代表性诗人的作品，如莎士比亚、斯宾塞、华兹华斯等，浅析选读诗歌中蕴含的思政主题。

第四章戏剧：介绍戏剧的起源和戏剧的种类，讨论戏剧的要素（矛盾、对话以及主题），选读并赏析代表戏剧家的作品，如莎士比亚，萧伯纳、威廉姆斯，浅析戏剧并分析作品中蕴含的思政主题。

每个章节选读作品之后都附上了思考题，旨在提升学生的英语文学鉴赏能力，培养学生的英语批判思维。

本书是西南林业大学"十四五规划教材"建设项目、西南林业大学外国语学院学科点建设项目以及西南林业大学第二批"SPOC"课程建设《英语文学导论》项目阶段成果。晏玉屏老师负责第一、二章的编写和大纲的制定以及内容审定工作，姜泽卫老师负责第三、四章的编写，楚承华老师负责内容审定工作。本书适合大学英语专业本科阶段的学习者以及热爱英美文学的社会人士。教材的内容是编者们在日常教学过程中，依据学生的学习特点选取，作品的思政分析是编者们在日常文学教学中积累所得，由于编者的理论水平和学术水平有限，在编写过程中存在欠妥之处，请广大读者们不吝指教。

编　者

2023 年 10 月

目　　录

Introduction

As the title of this book denotes, the authors concentrate on English literature, concerning the three types of literature in Anglo-American literary world: fiction, poetry and drama. Taking the academic fashion into consideration, with great efforts of the authors, this book selects the following topics for discussion: the genre, the elements of the genre, classical authors and their literary works. What's more, in each chapter, the authors try to probe into the ideological and political elements in the selective readings. Study and discussion questions are set at the end of each chapter. The purpose of this book is to connect closely the appreciation of literary works with the perfection of students' personalities.

Before we begin the discussion on the three genres of English literature, it is essential for us to get to know some basic questions: What is literature? What are the types or genres of literary works? What is the relationship between English literature and moral education?

Unit 1　What is Literature?

The word "**literature**" came into English from the 14th century in the sense of polite learning through reading. A man of literature, or a man of letters, meant what we would now describe as a man of wide reading. So, this word corresponds mainly to the modern meaning of the word "literacy". From the mid-18th century, literature referred to the practice and profession of writing. It appears to be closely connected with the heightened self-consciousness of the profession of author-ship. Since the 19th century, literature has been the high skills of writing in the special context of high imagination.

We can define literature as language artistically used to achieve identifiable literary qualities and to convey meaningful messages. Literature is the record of human history. All human experience has been described in it: the sweetest love, the most heartbroken betrayal, the most ferocious war, the hardest struggle, the joyful laughter and the miserable cry, the most precious friendship, and the fiercest hatred and revenge.

Literature means imaginative writings that are valued as works of art, writing which is not literally true. According to *(Longman Dictionary of Contemporary English)* literature means books, plays, poems, etc., that people think are important and good, It accounts the complexity of language and the words variety of written texts. Some define literature as writing which is "imaginative" or fictive, as opposed to factual, true, or historical.

To the Russian formalists, literature is a particular organization of language, which has its own laws, structures and devices. It should exist by itself rather than being reduced to something else. The claiming of the Russian formalists echoes with "Art for art's sake".

Literature is imitation. Aristotle pointed out that "Poetry in general seems to have sprung from two cases, each of them lying deep in our nature. First, the instinct of imitation is implanted in man from childhood, one difference between him and other animals being that he is the most imitative of living creatures and through imitation learns his earliest lessons; and no less universal is the pleasure felt in things imitated…" (Aristotle, 1997).

Literature is function. Socrates contends that "The effect of good poetry is to lead the youth to follow the correct path permitted by the law and in agreement with the experience of the elders." Philip Sydney and Samuel Johnson, all stress the instructive role of literature. They hold that literature must be entertaining and pleasing although the ultimate goal is to instruct.

Great works of literature enable us to study the way in which people live out their social roles. Literature shows not only the socialized behavior of individuals, but also the process of their socialization as well; it speaks not only of individual experience, but also of the meaning of that experience. Therefore, a writer is a specialized thinker about the individual. Writers are sometimes people with visionary or prophetic insight into human life. All of us who read literature will find our knowledge of human affairs broadened and deepened whether in the individual, the social, the racial, or the international sphere. We shall understand the possibility of human life, both for good and evil; we shall understand how we came to live at a particular time and place, with all its pleasures and vexations and problems; we shall understand the ways onwards which are open to us, and we shall perhaps be able to make right rather than wrong choices.

Unit 2　Genres of Literature

Literature comes from human interest in telling a story, in arranging words in artistic forms, in describing in words some aspects of our human experiences. This human activity embodies human desire to express and share experiences. At the beginning, the literary impulse exists only in one's mind. It is the writer who turns this impulse into literature: a story, a poem, a play, or an essay, with the medium of language. It is a writer's "performance in words" as Robert Frost once said. There are mainly four types of literature: fiction, poetry, drama and essay. In this book, the authors mainly introduce the former three types in details in the successive three chapters.

Fiction. In an inclusive sense, fiction is any literary narrative, whether in prose or verse, which is invented instead of being an account of events that in fact happen. In a narrower sense, fiction denotes only narratives that are written in prose (the novel and short story), and sometimes is used simply as a synonym for the novel. In the very first paragraph of their book *Understanding Fiction*, Cleanth Brooks and Robert Penn Warren said: "As soon as the cave man had leisure to sit around the fire while darkness covered the world beyond, fiction was born. In words, he relived shivering with fear or gloating in victory, the events of the hunt; he recounted the past history of the tribe; he narrated the deeds of heroes and men of cunning; he told the marvels; he struggled in myths to explain the world and fate; he glorified himself in daydreams converted to narrative" (Brooks, 1988).

Generally speaking, a fiction goes back to the prehistorical times. It is a kind of impulse in recounting some events real or imagined. The passion to recount these human experiences and the desire to narrate these stories are recorded in fictions we read nowadays. We read these fictions with just as much interest as the fireside cavemen listened to their stories, as they embody some of our basic interests, needs and desires buried deep in the human psyche.

Poetry. In broad sense, poetry means poems in general or the art of writing poems. A piece of poem expresses emotions, experiences, and ideas, especially in short lines using words that rhyme. According to Aristotle: "Poetry, therefore, is more philosophical and of higher value than history; for poetry tends to express the universe, history, the particular" (Adams, 1971). For Aristotle, poetry is a species of mimesis, which is imitation. Poetry uses different mediums, objects, and modes to carry out an imitation. In his *Defense for Poetry*, Philip Sydney points out that the chief end of poetry is to teach or delight. He values poetry over history, law and philosophy. Sydney goes further than Aristotle: Poetry, above all the other arts and sciences, embodies truth. Sydney's ideas about poetry finds resonance with Samuel Johnson's understanding of poetry: The end of writing is to instruct; the end of writing poetry is to instruct by pleasing. William Wordsworth says: "Poetry is the breath and finer spirit of all knowledge." He specially values the emotional function of poetry. In the Preface to *Lyrical Ballads*, Wordsworth assumes that poetry is the spontaneous overflow of powerful feelings: it takes its origin for emotion recollected in tranquility. On the contrary, T.S. Eliot points out that "Poetry is not a tuning loose of emotion, but an escape from emotion; it is not the expression of personality, but an escape from personality. But of course, only those who have personality and emotions know what it means to want to escape from these things" (常耀信, 2008).

Based on the above disparate discussion about poetry, it is hard to give a specific definition to poetry. However, all the poetry can be appreciated in terms of the basic elements in poetry. The basic elements in a poetry usually consist of voice, tone, diction, syntax, imagery, figure of speech, rhyme, rhythm sound, theme and so on.

Drama. The form of composition is designed for performance in the theatre, in which actors take the roles of characters, perform the indicated action, and utter the written dialogue. The common alternative name for a dramatic composition is a play. Aristotle defined drama as "imitated human action". *Modern Webster* defined drama as: a composition in verse or prose intended to portray life or character or to tell a story usually involving conflicts and emotions through action and dialogue and typically designed for theatrical performance.

Western drama originated in Ancient Greece. Usually, people use two masks to symbolize drama: one laughing and one weeping. These masks signify traditional generic division between comedy and tragedy. The laughing mask stands for Thalia, the Muse of Comedy and the weeping mask stands for Melpomene, the Muses of Tragedy.

Essay. Essay is any short composition in prose that undertakes to discuss a matter, express a point of view, persuade us to accept a thesis on any subjects, or simply entertain. Essays can be divided into formal and informal ones. The formal essay, or article is relatively impersonal: the author writes as an authority, or at least as highly knowledgeable and expounds the subject in an orderly way. Examples can be found in various scholarly journals, as well as among the serious articles on current topics and issues in any of the magazines addressed to a thoughtful audience—*Harper's, Commentary, Scientific American,* and so on. In the informal essay, the author assumes a tone of intimacy with his audience, tends to deal with everyday things rather than with public affairs or specialized topics, and writes in a relaxed, self-revelatory, and sometimes whimsical fashion. Accessible modern examples are to be found in any issue of *The New Yorker*.

In the early nineteenth century the founding of new types of magazines, and their steady proliferation, gave great impetus to the writing of essays and made them a major department of literature. This was the age when William Hazlitt, Thomas De Quincey, Charles Lamb, and, later in the century, Robert Louis Stevenson brought the English essay, especially the personal essay, to a level that has not been surpassed. Major American essayists in the nineteenth century include Washington Irving, Emerson, Thoreau, James Russell Lowell, and Mark Twain. In the twentieth century, the many periodicals poured out scores of essays every week. Most of them were formal in type; Virginia Woolf, George Orwell, E.M. Forster, James Thurber, E.B. White, James Bald win, Joan Didion, Susan Sontag, and Toni Morrison, however, were notable twentieth-century practitioners of the informal essay.

Unit 3　Literature and Moral Education

The fundamental task of university is to strengthen the moral values and cultivate people, and its key lies not only in the morality lessons, but also in the curriculum of university. Under the guidance of the Ministry of Education, the proposal of moral education in all courses was first put into practice by universities in Shanghai in 2014 while taking the pilot educational reform work. In 2016, at "The National Conference on Moral Education in Colleges and Universities", Xi Jinping stressed the importance of moral education for in all the courses of universities and colleges. In May 2020, the Ministry of Education issued *The Guidance Outline for Moral Education in the Curriculum of Higher Education* (hereinafter referred to as the *Outline*). The *Outline* points out that we should comprehensively promote moral education in all universities and all subjects, to search the moralizing function of each subject, and improve the quality of students in colleges and universities. Under this background, various colleges and universities throughout the country have carried out the reform of teaching mode which deeply excavates the virtuous elements in the specialized curriculum, in order to achieve the goal of co-development with morality lessons.

Currently, foreign language learning is a bridge to realize communication between China and foreign countries. Foreign language teaching plays an important role in spreading Chinese culture, telling Chinese stories and dealing with foreign affairs. Foreign language courses involve philosophy, history, culture, literature and so on. The hidden function of moral education in the course of foreign language teaching cannot be ignored.

According to *The National Standard for Teaching Quality of Foreign Language and Literature Specialty in Ordinary Colleges of Higher Learning* (hereinafter referred to as National Standard), literature of foreign languages includes not only the literature of target countries, but also the world literature and critical theories, in which Chinese literature is involved. Specifically, it refers to the main writers 'works, as well as the literary movements, and artistic achievements in different periods throughout history, aiming to broaden the students' view.

Thus, literature of foreign languages emphasizes knowledge acquiring, ability fostering, and personality shaping. This book mainly introduces the three genres (fiction, poetry and drama) of Anglo-American literature, representative writers, analysis of classical literary works and moral issues implied in these works. The original reason for the birth of various literary genres was to serve the ruling class, such as English fiction. Modern English novel was initiated in the 18th century. In order to celebrate its glorious history of capital accumulation and overseas expansion, the new bourgeoisie created a new literary genre suitable for the middle-class people. Defoe's *Robinson Crusoe* is a typical example. Therefore, literary works, to a certain extent, contain the prevailing ideas of dominant social class.

While appreciating the beauty of western literature, learners might also be influenced by the thoughts of individualism, egoism and utilitarianism. University students are still in the process of shaping their views on life, world and values, while some thoughts contained in literary works will bring negative influence to their growth. The traditional teaching of Anglo-American literature often pays attention to literature itself, but ignores its recessive function in moral education. Echoing with the moral education mission of universities, we should absorb the essence of English literature, discard the worthless dross, and pay attention to cultivate students' competence in thinking, criticizing and aesthetic judgement.

Fiction

Unit 1　General Introduction to Fiction

As for prose fiction, Sir Philip Sydney, Renaissance statesman, poet and writer . wrote *Arcadia* in 1580, which is a pastoral romance of love and courtship. John Bunyan's *The Pilgrim's Progress* in 1678 is a religious prose allegory depicting the pilgrimage of a Christian in search of salvation. These prose fictions paved the way for the rise and maturity of the 18th century British novels.

The English term "novel" drives from the Italian word "novella" for "new", "news" or "short stories of something new". "Novel" was applied by Giovanni Boccaccio to the short prose narratives in his *The Decameron*. In a narrow sense, a novel is a realistic fiction, complete in itself and contains the essential elements of setting, theme, plot, character, etc. English novels originated from the combination of several traditional literary forms, involving medieval morality plays, religious sermons and allegorical stories. Spanish picaresque novels and French narrative prose also influenced the rise of the English novel in the 18th century. Cervantes' masterpiece *Don Quixote* was widely read, imitated and challenged by English novelists in the 18th century. The theme and motive of love and courtship in French Romance was also integrated into the English novels.

In his book *The Novel and the People*, Ralph Fox comments as follows: "The novel is the most important gift of bourgeois, or capitalist, civilization to the world's imaginative culture." Cervantes' *Don Quixote* marked the beginning of modern European novels, while modern English novels did not mature until the 18th century with the development of Industrial Revolution and the uprising bourgeois culture. The 18th century witnessed the triumph of capitalism and colonization in Britain. Because of their extravagance and deterioration, London theatres were closed down. Drama, once thriving in the Elizabeth Age, declined in the 18th Century. Thus, the thriving new social class called for a new pattern of literary works. The rising bourgeois class wanted to create a new kind of literature that could praise the bourgeois ideas, values, life styles and their heroic deeds. Besides, the rapid growth of a large middle-class reading public demanded a new literary form. With large amount of leisure time, the improvement of literacy, the booming of printing and the assistance of circulating libraries, the dominant middle-class people called for something easy, fun and practical to read which urged the birth of novels. The publication in the society had already shown the change of literary taste in the public. The 18th century saw the first publication of newspapers, periodical, trade reports, travel books and "true" accounts of how individual rose from poverty to wealth.

The representatives in this period were Daniel Defoe, Samuel Richardson and Henry Fielding. Defoe's *Robinson Crusoe* symbolized the beginning of modern novel. As the masterpiece of Defoe, it was based on a real fact. In 1704, Alexander Selkirk, a Scottish sailor, was marooned on the island of Juan Fernandez in the Atlantic, and lived there alone for four years. The story of his adventure aroused great interest in the public and Defoe took up the subject and wrote the novel. He interwove the story with many of his imaginations, which seemed to be a true story. *Robinson Crusoe* gained great popularity in that it told the ordinary life experience of the middle-class people and illustrated the heroic deeds and social values of their own.

The function of novels is to entertain and to instruct or educate. Like Samuel Richardson's *Pamela* and Henry Fielding's *Tom Jones,* both novels emphasized the importance of virtues and virtue reward. The 18th century English novels had three features: first, realism, which depicts the real things occurred in life; second, individualism, which emphasized the importance of individual; third, contemporaneity, which represents the daily experience of contemporary British people.

Unit 2　Story and Plot: Joseph Conrad's *The Lagoon*

2.1　Elements of Fiction: Story and Plot

The word "**story**" is a literary term means a series of events recorded in their chronological order. This is the way things happen. But a short story or a novel is not merely a recording of things. Writers usually select and reorganize the materials to form a pattern that is more than mere sequence of events, and that contains the authors' viewpoints and is meaningful to the readers. So "**plot**" is how the story is presented by deliberately re-organizing the chosen materials to reveal their dramatic, thematic and emotional significance. Plot is different from story: When we summarize the story in a literary work, we say that first this happens, then that, then that... . It is only when we specify how this is related to that, by cause and motivations, and in what ways all these matters are rendered, ordered, and organized so as to achieve their particular effects, that a synopsis begins to be adequate to the plot.

There are evidently a number of different ways one might go about discussing the concept of plot and its function in the range of narrative forms. Plot is, first of all, a constant of all written and oral narrative, in that a narrative without at least a minimal plot would be incomprehensible. Plot is the principle of inter connectedness and intention we cannot do without moving through the discrete elements like incidents, episodes, actions of a narrative.

There are a great variety of plot forms. For instance, some plots are designed to achieve tragic effects, and others to achieve the effects of comedy, romance, satire, or some other genre. The traditional plot consists of five parts: **beginning, rising conflict, climax, falling conflict, denouement (conclusion).** While, many modern and postmodern writers deliberately avoid cause-effect relations as they believe that well-plotted texts fail to render reality of life accurately. They seldom follow linear development and place fragments side by side with an open ending, making the structure of their works loosely plotted. The open ending leaves uncertainty and imagination room to the readers.

In fiction, there are not merely one plot. Different plots weave in one literary work. The one plays the dominant part is called main plot and others are called subplots.

2.2　Joseph Conrad and His Literary Life

Joseph Conrad (1857—1924), one of the most original novelists of early 20th century, was a pole by birth. He had a two-decade-long sea wandering and a twenty-year-long literary career. His early Polish life and his overseas journeys had left a life-long imprint on his thought and writing as he believed that "a novelist lives in his work".

Poland had been dismembered by Czarist Russia, Prussia and Austria since the 18th century. Conrad's father was arrested and sent into exile to icy North Russia for his participation in the anti-Russian uprising of 1863—1864. Four-year-old Conrad and his mother followed him in exile. Conrad's parents died within four years and he was brought up by his maternal uncle who continued to influence him as a patriot. Conrad's early experience of Poland fostered in him a sense of justice and that subconsciously underlay influence his writings.

Conrad' s overseas journeys, especially his trip to Congo, had a great impact on him. He made his important trip in 1890 when he sailed along the Congo River for four months. He was shocked by the horror, chaos and cruelty caused by the "civilized whites" in Congo. Conrad' s Congo experience was a turning point in his life, re-steering him from a sailor to a writer, his attitude from pride in British power to doubt about European colonialism, and reforming him from "a mere animal" to a merciful man who abhorred oppression.

Conrad used his life experience as the first-hand material for his writing career. Throughout his life, he completed 36 novels, two volumes of memoirs and 28 short stories. In terms of plot and setting, most of his writings are classified as sea and jungle novels, including Youth, Typhoon, Within the Tides, Almayer's Folly, The Nigger of the Narcissus, The Black Mate, An Outposts of Progress, Lord Jim, Heart of Darkness, Nostromo, The Secret Agent and Under the Western Eyes. In all his writings, Conrad intended to expose the depths of the human soul in the chaotic world in face of adversity, moral or political.

2.3　Introduction to *The Lagoon*

"The Lagoon" is a short story by Joseph Conrad composed in 1896 and first published in *Cornhill Magazine* in 1897. As is mentioned at the beginning of this chapter, the word "**story**" is a literary term means a series of events recorded in their chronological order; while the word "plot" tells how the story is presented by deliberately re-organizing the chosen materials to reveal their dramatic, thematic and emotional significance. According to its chronological order, the story of "Lagoon" is about a white man, referred to as "Tuan" (the equivalent of "Lord" or "Sir"), who is traveling through an Indonesia rainforest and is forced to stop for the night with a distant Malay friend named Arsat. Upon arriving, he finds Arsat distraught, for his lover is dying. Arsat tells the distant and rather silent white man a story of his past.

The story told by Arsat is a story within a story. He started with the time when he and his brother (the brother was never given a name) kidnapped Diamelen (Arsat's wife, who was previously a servant of the Rajah's wife). They all fled in a boat at night and traveled until they were exhausted. They stopped on a bit of land jutting out into the water to rest. Soon however, they spotted a large boat of the Rajah's men coming to find them. Arsat's brother told Diamelen and Arsat to flee to the other side, where there was a fisherman's hut. He instructed them to take the fisherman's boat and then stayed back, telling them to wait for him, while he tried to hold the pursuers off with a limited amount of gunpowder. Arsat then started pushing the canoe from shore, leaving his brother behind. He then saw his brother running down the path, being chased by the pursuers. Arsat's brother tripped and the enemy was upon him. His brother got up, then called out to him three times, but Arsat never looked back. The pursuers killed his brother and Arsat had betrayed his brother for the woman he loved, who was now dying.

Then, the author comes back from the memory of Arsat. Towards the end of the story, symbolically, the sun rose and Diamelen died. With Diamelen's death, Arsat had nothing because he lost his brother and wife. He told Tuan he planned to return to his home village to avenge his brother's death. The story concludes with Tuan's simply leaving, and Arsat's staring dejectedly into the sun and "a world of illusion".

In plot, authors usually reorganize the deliberately chosen material to create dramatic effect and gain emotional significance. In " The Lagoon", the author adopts flashback at the beginning to create a suspense for readers. The white man acts just as a listener without giving any meaningful remarks. The short story can be divided into three parts. In the first part, the white man, Tuan, arrived at the dwelling of Arsat and found Arsat's dying wife. In the second part, the Arsat then acts as a storyteller in recalling his eloping with Diamelen with the help of his brother and his brother's death caused by Rajah's men. In the third part, which is also the climax of the story, Diamelen died, and Arsat decided to avenge his brother's death. The author deliberately disorganizes the chronological order to create suspense and dramatic significance.

2.4　Selected Readings

The Lagoon

The white man, leaning with both arms over the roof of the little house in the stern of the boat, said to the steersman:

"We will pass the night in Arsat's clearing. It is late."

The Malay only grunted, and went on looking fixedly at the river. The white man rested his chin on his crossed arms and gazed at the wake of the boat. At the end of the straight avenue of forests cut by the intense glitter of the river, the sun appeared unclouded and dazzling, poised low over the water that shone smoothly like a ban of metal. The forests, sombre and dull, stood motionless and silent on each side of the broad stream. At the foot of big, towering trees, trunkless **nipa palms**[1] rose from the mud of the bank, in bunches of leaves enormous and heavy, that hung unstirring over the brown swirl of eddies. In the stillness of the air every tree, every leaf, every bough, every tendril of creeper and every petal of **minute**[2] blossoms seemed to have been bewitched into an immobility perfect and final. Nothing moved on the river but the eight paddles that rose flashing regularly, dipped together with a single splash while the steersman swept right and left with a periodic and sudden flourish of his blade describing a glinting semicircle above his head. The **churned-up**[3] water frothed alongside with a confused murmur. And the white man's canoe, advancing upstream in the short-lived disturbance of its own making, seemed to enter the portals of a land from which the very memory of motion had forever departed.

The white man, turning his back upon the setting sun, looked along the empty and broad expanse of the sea-reach. For the last three miles of its course the wandering, hesitating river, as if enticed irresistibly by the freedom of an open horizon, flows straight into the sea, flows straight to the east—to the east that harbours both light and darkness. Astern of the boat the repeated call of some bird, a cry discordant and feeble, skipped along over the smooth water and lost itself, before it could reach the other shore, in the breathless silence of the world.

The steersman dug his paddle into the stream, and held hard with stiffened straight reach seemed to pivot on its center, the forests swung in a semicircle, arms, his body thrown forward. The water gurgled aloud; and suddenly the long straight reach seemed to pivot on its center, the forest swung in a semicircle, and the slanting beams of sunset touched the broadside of the canoe with a fiery glow, throwing the slender and distorted shadows of its crew upon the streaked glitter of the river. The white man turned to look ahead. The course of the boat had been altered at right-angles to the stream, and the carved dragon-head of its prow was pointing now at a gap in the fringing bushes of the bank. It glided through brushing the overhanging twigs, and disappeared from the river like some slim and amphibious creature leaving the water for its **lair**[4] in the forests.

The narrow creek was like a ditch: tortuous, fabulously deep; filled with gloom under the thin strip of pure and shining blue of the heaven Immense trees soared up, invisible behind the **festooned draperies**[5] of creepers. Here and there, near the glistening blackness of the water, a twisted root of some tall tree showed amongst the **tracery**[6] of small ferns, black and dull, writhing and motionless, like an arrested snake. The short words of the paddlers reverberated loudly between the thick and sombre walls of vegetation. Darkness oozed out from between the trees, through the tangled maze of the creepers, from behind the great fantastic and unstirring leaves; the darkness, mysterious and invincible; the darkness scented and poisonous of impenetrable forests.

The men poled in the **shoaling**[7] water. The creek broadened, opening out into a wide sweep of a stagnant lagoon. The forests receded from the marshy bank, leaving a level strip of bright green, reedy grass to frame the reflected blueness of the sky. A fleecy pink cloud drifted high above, trailing the delicate colouring of its image under the floating leaves and the silvery blossoms of the lotus. A little house, perched on high piles, appeared black in the distance. Near it two tall **nibong palms**[8], that seemed to have come out of the forests in the background leaned slightly over the ragged roof, with a suggestion of sad tenderness and care in the droop of their leafy and soaring heads.

The steersman, pointing with his paddle, said, "Arsat is there. I see his canoe **fast**[9] between the piles."

The polers ran along the sides of the boat glancing over their shoulders at the end of the day's journey. They would have preferred to spend the night somewhere else than on this lagoon of weird aspect and ghostly reputation. Moreover, they disliked Arsat, first as a stranger and also because he who repairs a ruined house, and dwells in it, proclaims that he is not afraid to live amongst the spirits that haunt the places abandoned by mankind. Such a man can disturb the course of fate by glances or words; while his familiar ghosts are not easy to **propitiate**[10] by **casual wayfarers**[11] upon whom they long to wreak the malice of their human master White men care not for such things, being unbelievers and in league with the Father of Evil, who lead them unharmed through the invisible dangers of this world. To the warnings of the righteous they oppose an offensive pretense of disbelief What is there to be done?

So they thought, throwing their weight on the end of their long poles. The big canoe glided on swiftly, noiselessly, and smoothly, towards Arsat's clearing, till, in a great rattling of poles thrown down, and the loud murmurs of "Allah be praised!" it came with a gentle knock against the crooked piles below the house.

The boatmen with uplifted faces shouted discordantly "Arsat! O Arsat!" Nobody came. The white man began to climb the rude ladder giving access to the bamboo platform before the house. The **juragan**[12] of the boat said sulkily, "We will cook in the sampan, and sleep on the water."

"Pass my blankets and the basket," said the white man, curtly.

He knelt on the edge of the platform to receive the bundle. Then the boat shoved off, and the white man, standing up, confronted Arsat, who had come out through the low door of his hut. He was a man young, powerful, with broad chest and muscular arms. He had nothing on but his **sarong**[13]. His head was bare. His big, soft eyes stared eagerly at the white man, but his voice and **demeanour**[14] were composed as he asked, without any words of greeting:

"Have you medicine, **Tuan**[15]?"

"No," said the visitor in a startled tone. "No. Why? Is there sickness in the house?" "Enter and see," replied Arsat in the same calm manner and turning short round, passed again through the small doorway. The white man dropping his bundles, followed.

In the dim light of the dwelling he made out on a couch of bamboos a woman stretched on her back under a broad sheet of red cotton cloth. She lay still, as if dead; but her big eyes, wide open, glittered in the gloom, staring upwards at the slender rafters, motionless and unseeing. She was in a high fever and evidently unconscious. Her cheeks were sunk slightly, her lips were partly open and on the young face there was the ominous and fixed expression—the absorbed, contemplating expression of the unconscious who are going to die. The two men stood looking down at her in silence.

"Has she been long ill?" asked the traveler.

"I have not slept for five nights" answered the Malay, in a deliberate tone. At first she heard voices calling her from the water and struggled against me who held her. But since the sun of today rose she hears nothing—she hears not me. She sees not me—me!

He remained silent for a minute, then asked softly:

"Tuan, will she die?"

"I fear so," said the white man, sorrowfully. He had known Arsat years ago, in a far country in times of trouble and danger, when no friendship is to be despised. And since his Malay friend had come unexpectedly to dwell in the hut on the lagoon with a strange woman, he had slept many times there, in his journeys up and down the river.

He liked the man who knew how to keep faith in council and how to fight without fear by the side of his white friend. He liked him—not so much perhaps as a man likes his favourite dog- but still he liked him well enough to help and ask no questions, to think sometimes vaguely and hazily in the midst of his own pursuits, about the lonely man and the long-haired woman with audacious face and triumphant eyes, who lived together hidden by the forests—alone and feared.

The white man came out of the hut in time to see the enormous conflagration of sunset put out by the swift and stealthy shadows that, rising like a black and impalpable vapour above the tree-tops, spread over the heaven, extinguishing the crimson glow of floating clouds and the red brilliance of departing daylight. In a few moments all the stars came out above the intense blackness of the earth and the great lagoon gleaming suddenly with reflected lights resembled an oval patch of night sky flung down into the hopeless and abysmal night of the wilderness. The white man had some supper out of the basket then collecting a few sticks that lay about the platform, made up a small fire not for warmth but for the sake of the smoke, which would keep off the mosquitoes. He wrapped himself in the blankets and sat with his back against the reed wall of the house, smoking thoughtfully.

Arsat came through the doorway with noiseless steps and squatted down by the fire. The white man moved his outstretched legs a little.

"She breathes," said Arsat in a low voice, anticipating the expected question. "She breathes and burns as if with a great fire. She speaks not; she hears not -and burns!"

He paused for a moment, then asked in a quiet, **incurious**[16] tone:

"Tuan ... will she die?"

The white man moved his shoulders uneasily and muttered in a hesitating manner:

"If such is her fate."

"No, Tuan," Arsat said, calmly "If such is my fate. I hear, I see, I wait. I remember... Tuan, do you remember the old days? Do you remember my brother?"

"Yes," said the white man. The Malay rose suddenly and went in. The other sitting still outside, could hear the voice in the hut. Arsat said: "Hear me! Speak!" words were succeeded by a complete silence. "O Diamelen!" He cried, suddenly. After that cry there was a deep sigh. Arsat came out and sank down again in his old place.

They sat in silence before the fire. There was no sound within the house, there was no sound near them; but far away on the lagoon they could hear the voices of the boatmen ringing fitful and distinct on the calm water. The fire in the bows of the sampan shone faintly in the distance with a hazy red glow. Then it died out. The voices ceased. The land and the water slept invisible, unstirring and mute. It was as though there had been nothing left in the world but the glitter of stars streaming, ceaseless and vain, through the black stillness of the night.

The white man gazed straight before him into the darkness with wide-open eyes. The fear and fascination, the inspiration and the wonder of death—of death near, unavoidable, and unseen, soothed the unrest of his race and stirred the most indistinct, the most intimate of his thoughts. The ever-ready suspicion of evil, the **gnawing**[17] suspicion that lurks in our hearts, flowed out into the stillness round him -into the stillness profound and dumb, and made it appear untrustworthy and infamous, like the **placid**[18] and impenetrable mask of an unjustifiable violence. In that **fleeting**[19] and powerful disturbance of his being the earth enfolded in the starlight peace became a shadowy country of inhuman strife a battle-field of phantoms terrible and charming, **august**[20] or ignoble, struggling ardently for the possession of our helpless hearts. An unquiet and mysterious country of inextinguishable desires and fears.

A **plaintive**[21] murmur rose in the night; a murmur saddening and startling, as if the great solitudes of surrounding woods had tried to whisper into his ear the wisdom of their immense and lofty indifference. Sounds hesitating and vague floated in the air round him, shaped themselves slowly into words; and at last flowed on gently in a murmuring stream of soft and monotonous sentences. He stirred like a man waking up and changed his position slightly. Arsat, motionless and shadow sitting with bowed head under the stars, was speaking in a low and dreamy tone:

"...for where can we lay down the heaviness of our trouble but in a friend's heart? A man must speak of war and of love. You, Tuan, know what war is, and you have seen me in time of danger seek death as other men seek life! A writing may be lost, a life may be written; but what the eye has seen is truth and remains in the mind!"

"I remember," said the white man. Quietly, Arsat went on with mournful composure.

"Therefore, I shall speak to you of love. Speak in the night. Speak before both night and love are gone—and the eye of day looks upon my sorrow and my shame; upon my blackened face; upon my bunt-up heart."

A sigh, short and faint, marked an almost imperceptible pause, and then his words flowed on, without a stir, without a gesture.

"After the time of trouble and war was over and you went away from my country in the pursuit of your desires, which we, men of the islands, cannot understand, I and my brother became again, as we had been before, the sword-bearers of the Ruler. You know we were men of family belonging to a ruling race, and more fit than any to carry on our right shoulder the emblem of power. And in the time of prosperity, Si Dendring showed us favour, as we, in time of sorrow, had showed to him the faithfulness of our courage. It was a time of peace. A time of deer-hunts and cock- fights; of idle talks and foolish squabbles between men whose bellies are full and weapons are rusty. But the sower watched the young rice-shoots grow up without fear, and the traders came and went, departed lean and returned fat into the river of peace. They brought news, too. Brought lies and truth mixed together, so that no man knew when to rejoice and when to be sorry. We heard from them about you also. They had seen you here and had seen you there. And I was glad to hear, for I remembered the stirring times, and I always remembered you, Tuan, till the time came when my eyes could see nothing in the past, because they had looked upon the one who is dying there—in the house."

He stopped to exclaim in an intense whisper,"O **Mara bahia**[22]! O Calamity!" then went on speaking a little louder!

"There's no worse enemy and no better friend than a brother, Tuan, for one brother knows another, and in perfect knowledge is strength for good or evil. I loved my brother. I went to him and told him that I could see nothing but one face, hear nothing but one voice. He told me: 'Open your heart so that she can see what is in it -and wait. Patience is wisdom. Inchi Midah may die or our Ruler may throw off his fear of a woman!'... I waited!... You remember the lady with the veiled fan, Tuan, and the fear of our Ruler before her cunning and temper. And if she wanted her servant, what could I do? But I fed the hunger of my heart on short glances and stealthy words. I loitered on the path to the bath-houses in the daytime, and when the sun had fallen behind the forest I crept along the jasmine hedges of the women's courtyard. Unseeing, we spoke to one another through the scent of flowers, through the veil of leaves, through the blades of long grass that stood still before our lips so great was our prudence, so faint was the murmur of our great longing. The time passed swiftly ... and there were whispers amongst women—and our enemies watched—my brother was gloomy and I began to think of killing and of a fierce death.... . We are of a people who take what they want—like you whites. There is time when a man should forget loyalty and respect. Mighty and authority are given to rulers, but to all men is given love and strength and courage. My brother said, 'You shall take her from their midst. We are two who are like one.' And I answered, 'Let it be soon, for I find no warmth in sunlight that does not shine upon her'. Our time came when the Ruler and all the great people went to the mouth of the river to fish by torchlight. There were hundreds of boats, and on the white sand, between the water and the forests, dwellings of leaves were built for the households of the **Rajahs**[23]. The smoke of cooking-fires was like a blue mist of the evening, and many voices rang in it joyfully While they were making the boats ready to beat up the fish, my brother came to me and said, 'To-night!' I looked to my weapons, and when the time came our canoe took its place in the circle of boats carrying the torches. The lights blazed on the water, but behind the boats there was darkness. When the shouting began and the excitement made them like mad we dropped out. The water swallowed our fire and we floated back to the shore that was dark with only here and there the glimmer of embers. We could hear the talk of slave-girls amongst the sheds.

Then we found a place deserted and silent. We waited there. She came running along the shore, rapid and leaving no trace, like a leaf driven by the wind into the sea. My brother said gloomily, 'Go and take her; carry her into our boat.' I lifted her in my arms. She panted. Her heart was beating against my breast. I said 'I take you from those people. You came to the cry of my heart, but my arms take you into my boat against the will of the great!' 'It is right,' said my brother. 'We are men who take what we want and can hold it against many. We should have taken her in daylight.' I said 'Let us be off; for since she was in my boat I began to think of our Ruler's many men.' 'Yes. Let us be off,' said my brother. 'We are cast out and this boat is our country now—and the sea is our refuge.' He lingered with his foot on the shore, and I entreated him to hasten, for I remembered the strokes of her heart against my breast and thought that two men cannot withstand a hundred. We left, paddling downstream close to the bank; and as we passed by the creek where they were fishing, the great shouting had ceased, but the murmur of voices was loud like the humming of insects flying at noonday. The boats floated, clustered together, in the red light of torches, under a black roof of smoke; and men talked of their sport. Men that boasted, and praised and jeered—men that would have been our friends in the morning, but on that night were already our enemies. We paddled swiftly past. We had no more friends in the country of our birth. She sat in the middle of the canoe with covered face; silent as she is now; unseeing as she is now—and I had no regret at what I was leaving because I could hear her breathing close to me—as I can hear her now."

He paused, listened with his ear turned to the doorway, then shook his head and went on: "My brother wanted to shout the cry of challenge—one cry only—to let the people know we were freeborn robbers who trusted our arms and the great sea.　And again I begged him in the name of our love to be silent. Could I not hear her breathing close to me? I knew the pursuit would come quick enough. My brother loved me. He dipped his paddle without a splash. He only said, 'There is half a man in you now—the other half is in that woman. I can wait when you are a whole man again, you will come back with me here to shout defiance. We are sons of the same mother.' I made no answer. All my strength and all my spirit were in my hands that held the paddle—for I longed to be with her in a safe place beyond the reach of men's anger and of women's spite. My love was so great, that I thought it could guide me to a country where death was unknown, if I could only escape from Inchi Midah's fury and from our Ruler's sword. We paddled with haste, breathing through our teeth. The blades bit deep into the smooth water. We passed out of the river; we flew in clear channels amongst the shallows. We skirted the black coast; we skirted the sand beaches where the sea speaks in whispers to the land; and the gleam of white sand flashed back past our boat, so swiftly she ran upon the water. We spoke not. Only once I said, 'Sleep Diamelen, for soon you may want all your strength.' I heard the sweetness of her voice, but I never turned my head. The sun rose and still we went on. Water fell from my face like rain from a cloud. We flew in the light and heat. I never looked back, but I knew that my brother's eyes, behind me, were looking steadily ahead, for the boat went as straight as a bushman's dart, when it leaves the end of the **sumpitan**[24].There was no better paddler, no better steersman than my brother. Many times, together, we had won races in that canoe. But we never had put out our strength as we did then—then, when for the last time we paddled together! There was no braver or stronger man in our country than my brother. I could not spare the strength to turn my head and look at him, but every moment I heard the hiss of his breath getting louder behind me. Still he did not speak. The sun was high. The heat clung to my back like a flame of fire. My ribs were ready to burst, but I could no longer get enough air into my chest. And then I felt I must cry out with my last breath, 'Let us rest!'… 'Good!' he answered; and his voice was firm. He was strong. He was brave. He knew not fear and no fatigue... My brother!"

A murmur powerful and gentle, a murmur vast and faint; the murmur of trembling leaves, of stirring boughs, ran through the tangled depths of the forests ran over the starry smoothness of the lagoon, and the water between the piles lapped the slimy timber once with a sudden splash. A breath of warm air touched the two men's faces and passed on with a mournful sound—a breath loud and short like an uneasy sigh of the dreaming earth.

Arsat went on in an even, low voice.

"We ran our canoe on the white beach of a little bay close to a long tongue of land that seemed to bar our road; a long-wooded cape going far into the sea. My brother knew that place. Beyond the cape a river has its entrance, and through the jungle of that land there is a narrow path. We made a fire and cooked rice. Then we lay down to sleep on the soft sand in the shade of our canoe, while she watched. No sooner had I closed my eyes than I heard her cry of alarm. We leaped up. The sun was halfway down the sky already, and coming in sight in the opening of the bay we saw a **prau**[25] manned by many paddlers. We knew it at once; it was one of our Rajah's praus. They were watching the shore, and saw us. They beat the gong, and turned the head of the prau into the bay. I felt my heart become weak within my breast. Diamelen sat on the sand and covered her face. There was no escape by sea. My brother laughed. He had the gun you had given him, Tuan, before you went away but there was only a handful of powder. He spoke to me quickly: 'Run with her along the path. I shall keep them back, for they have no firearms, and landing in the face of a man with a gun is certain death for some. Run with her. On the other side of that wood there is a fisherman's house —— and a canoe. When I have fired all the shots I will follow. I am a great runner, and before they can come up we shall be gone. I will hold out as long as I can, for she is but a woman—that can neither run nor fight but she has your heart in her weak hands.'He dropped behind the canoe. The prau was coming. She and I ran and as we rushed along the path, I heard shots. My brother fired once, twice… and the booming of the gong ceased. There was silence behind us. That neck of land is narrow. Before I heard my brother fire the third shot, I saw the shelving shore, and I saw the water again; the mouth of a broad river. We crossed a grassy glade. We ran down to the water. I saw a low hut above the black mud, and a small canoe hauled up. I heard another shot behind me. I thought, 'That is his last charge.' We rushed down to the canoe; a man came running from the hut, but I leaped on him, and we rolled together in the mud. Then I got up, and he lay still at my feet. I don't know whether l had killed him or not. I and Diamelen pushed the canoe afloat. I heard yells behind me and I saw my brother run across the glade. Many men were bounding after him. I took her in my arms and threw her into the boat, then leaped in myself. When I looked back I saw that my brother had fallen. He fell and was up again, but the men were closing round him. He shouted, 'I am coming!' The men were close to him. l looked. Many men. Then I looked at her. Tuan, I pushed the canoe! I pushed it into deep water. She was kneeling forward looking at me, and I said, 'Take your paddle,' while I struck the water with mine. Tuan, I heard him cry. I heard him cry my name twice; and I heard voices shouting. 'Kill! Strike!' I never turned back. I heard him calling my name again with a great shriek, as when life is going out together with the voice—and I never turned my head. My own name!.... My brother! Three times he called—but I was not afraid of life. Was she not there in that canoe? And could I not with her find a country where death is forgotten—where death is unknown!"

The white man sat up. Arsat rose and stood, an indistinct and silent figure above the dying embers of the fire. Over the lagoon a mist drifting and low had crept, erasing slowly the glittering images of the stars. And now a great expanse of white vapour covered the land: it flowed cold and gray in the darkness, eddied in noiseless whirls round the tree-trunks and about the platform of the house, which seemed to float upon a restless and impalpable illusion of a sea. Only far away the tops of the trees stood outlined on the twinkle of heaven, like a sombre and forbidding shore—a coast deceptive, pitiless and black.

Arsat's voice vibrated loudly in the profound peace.

"I had her there! I had her! To get her I would have faced all mankind. But I had her—and…"

His words went out ringing into the empty distances. He paused, and seemed to listen to them dying away very far—beyond help and beyond recall. Then he said quietly:

"Tuan, I loved my brother."

A breath of wind made him shiver. High above his head, high above the silent sea of mist the drooping leaves of the palms rattled together with a mournful and expiring sound. The white man stretched his legs. His chin rested on his chest, and he murmured sadly without lifting his head:

"We all love our brothers."

Arsat burst out with an intense whispering violence:

"What did I care who died? I wanted peace in my own heart."

He seemed to hear a stir in the house—listened—then stepped in noiselessly. The white man stood up. A breeze was coming in fitful puffs The stars shone paler as if they had retreated into the frozen depths of immense space. After a chill gust of wind, there were a few seconds of perfect calm and absolute silence. Then from behind the black and wavy line of the forests, a column of golden light shot up into the heavens and spread over the semicircle of the eastern horizon. The sun had risen. The mist lifted, broke into drifting patches, vanished into thin lying wreaths; and the unveiled lagoon lay polished and black, in the heavy shadows at the foot of the wall of trees. A white eagle rose over it with a slanting and ponderous fight, reached the clear sunshine and appeared dazzlingly brilliant for a moment, then soaring higher. became a dark and motionless speck before it vanished into the blue as if it had left the earth forever. The white man, standing gazing upwards before the doorway heard in the hut a confused and broken murmur of distracted words ending with a loud groan. Suddenly Arsat stumbled out with outstretched hands, shivered, and stood still for some time with fixed eyes. Then he said:

"She burns no more."

Before his face the sun showed its edge above the tree-tops rising steadily. The breeze freshened: a great brilliance burst upon the lagoon, sparkled on the rippling water. The forests came out of the clear shadows of the morning, became distinct, as if they had rushed nearer- to stop short in a great stir of leaves, of nodding boughs, of swaying branches. In the merciless sunshine the whisper of unconscious life grew louder, speaking in an incomprehensible voice round the dumb darkness of that human sorrow. Arsat's eyes wandered slowly. then stared at the rising sun.

"I can see nothing," he said half aloud to himself.

"There is nothing," said the white man, moving to the edge of the platform and waving his hand to his boat. A shout came faintly over the lagoon and the sampan began to glide towards the **abode**[26] of the friend of ghosts.

"If you want to come with me, I will wait all the morning," said the white man looking away upon the water.

"No, Tuan," said Arsat, softly. "I shall not eat or sleep in this house, but I must first see my road. Now I can see nothing—see nothing! There is no light and no peace in the world: but there is death—death for many. We are sons of the same mother—and I left him in the midst of enemies; but I am going back now."

He drew a long breath and went on in a dreamy tone:

"In a little while 1 shall see clear enough to strike—to strike. But she has died. and ... now...darkness."

He flung his arms wide open, let them fall along his body then stood still with unmoved face and stony eyes, staring at the sun. The white man got down into his canoe. The polers ran smartly along the sides of the boat, looking over their shoulders at the beginning of a weary journey. High in the stern, his head muffled up in white rags, the juragan sat moody letting his paddle trail in the water. The white man, leaning with both arms over the grass roof of the little cabin, looked back at the shining ripple of the boat's wake. Before the sampan passed out of the lagoon in the creek he lifted his eyes. Arsat had not moved. He stood lonely in the searching sunshine; and he looked beyond the great light of a cloudless day into the darkness of a world of illusions.

Notes

1.　nipa palms：聂帕榈

2.　minute：微小的；精细的

3.　churned-up：像（由搅拌器）搅拌过的；泛泡沫的

4.　lair：（野兽的）巢穴

5.　festooned draperies：挂着花彩的饰幔

6.　tracery：花饰窗格

7.　shoaling：（水等）变浅的；变成浅滩的

8.　nibong palms：巴雅椰

9.　fast：牢牢地、紧紧地（系在、固定在……上）

10.　propitiate：劝慰；抚慰

11.　casual wayfarers：不经意的旅人；没有固定目的的旅行者

12.　juragan：主人

13.　sarong：（马来人不分男女式样的）莎笼；围裙

14.　demeanour：行为；举止

15.　Tuan：（马来语）老爷；先生

16.　incurious：没有好奇心的；漠然的；不关心的

17.　gnawing：噬咬着；折磨人的；令人痛苦的

18.　placid：平静的；平和的

19.　fleeting：飞逝的；短暂的

20.　august：威严的；庄严的

21.　plaintive：哀婉的；悲伤的

22.　Mara bahia：灾难

23.　Rajahs：马来、爪哇等地的酋长、首领；印度的国王或王子

24.　sumpitan：毒矢吹管（婆罗洲人用的）

25. prau：（马来人的）狭长的快速帆船

26. abodes：住所；住处

Questions for discussion:

1. What may be the symbolic significance of "darkness" in this short story?

2. How will you describe the white man's attitude towards Arsat?

3. Joseph Conrad was one of the few British novelists who tried to portray positively non-European characters at the turn of the 20th century. Do you think he succeeded in doing it here?

2.5　Appreciation of Selected Readings

短篇小说《礁湖》（*The Lagoon*）描写了东南亚的马来亚丛林。作者采用了外景与心境交融的写作手法，通过对海洋丛林等原始场景的渲染和描写凸现人物的内心世界：如人对于大自然未知领域的征服欲望，未受到"文明"影响的人类的质朴的情感和敢爱敢恨的果敢、无畏。尤其是对于故事中"哥哥"的形象的刻画：忠诚善良，无私，珍视手足之情。从形式上看，故事完全由阿萨特（Arsat）叙述，"白人"在故事中完全是一个听众。小说中也能读出殖民主义色彩的味道，如在描述"白人"对阿萨特怀有的情感时，作者是这样写的："He liked him—not so much perhaps as a man likes his favourite dog…""他喜欢他——也许还没有一个人对自己的狗喜欢得那么深……"，而且还强调他们的友谊之所以开始，是因为当时"白人"的处境容不得他去"鄙视任何友谊"。

殖民主义色彩隐蔽在文章的背后，作者真正想要表达的是对于人性的思考。阿萨特爱上了首领夫人的女仆，哥哥则鼓励他要为爱情和自由不惜一切，要藐视权威，敢于向命运反抗。同时，哥哥也倾尽全力去帮助弟弟追求幸福甚至付出了生命的代价。出于对爱情和求生的本能，阿萨特却眼睁睁地看着哥哥被首领的大队人马杀死，放弃为哥哥争取一线生机的机会，头也不回地把船开走了。

阿萨特在故事中讲述了当自己面临欲望与亲人的命运，爱情与亲情产生冲突时，出于本能地选择了背叛。故事中，他饱受失去亲人与爱人的双重煎熬，最终从背叛、痛苦走向良知的觉醒。故事再次唤起读者的思考：人性本恶还是人性本善？

阿萨特出于本能和欲望选择弃哥哥而不顾，更深层次的原因是受西方长期盛行的利己主义（egoism）思想的影响。阿萨特把自己叙述成一位为了爱情而抛弃亲情、敢于反抗权威的勇士形象，却是建立在哥哥为他牺牲生命的基础之上。他所追求的爱情也是从自己的立场出发，阿萨特的妻子（Diamelen）在整个故事中都没有发声。作者甚至都没有提到 Diamelen 对于阿萨特的情感回应。她就像是一件被阿萨特掳走的战利品，毫无自主权。在故事的结尾，阿萨特落得了失去亲情和爱情的悲惨下场。归根结底，造成悲剧的原因是阿萨特的自私和欲望。

2.6　Supplementary Reading

Preface to *The Nigger of the "Narcissus"* (1897)

by Joesph Conrad

A work that aspires, however humbly, to the condition of art should carry its justification in every line. And art itself may be defined as a single-minded attempt to render the highest kind of justice to the visible universe, by bringing to light the truth, manifold and one, underlying its every aspect. It is an attempt to find in its forms, in its colours, in its light, in its shadows, in the aspects of matter and in the facts of life what of each is fundamental, what is enduring and essential—their one illuminating and convincing quality—the very truth of their existence. The artist, then, like the thinker or the scientist, seeks the truth and makes his appeal.

[…]

Confronted by the same enigmatical spectacle the artist descends within himself, and in that lonely region of stress and strife, if he be deserving and fortunate, he finds the terms of his appeal. His appeal is made to our less obvious capacities: to that part of our nature which, because of the warlike conditions of existence, is necessarily kept out of sight within the more resisting and hard qualities-like the vulnerable body within a steel armor. His appeal is less loud, more profound, less distinct, more stirring—and sooner forgotten. Yet its effect endures forever. The changing wisdom of successive generations discards ideas, questions facts, demolishes theories. But the artist appeals to that part of our being which is not dependent on wisdom; to that in us which is a gift and not an acquisition—and, therefore, more permanently enduring. He speaks to our capacity for delight and wonder, to the sense of mystery surrounding our lives; to our sense of pity, and beauty, and pain; to the latent feeling of fellowship with all creation—and to the subtle but invincible conviction of solidarity that knits together the loneliness of innumerable hearts, to the solidarity in dreams, in joy, in sorrow, in aspirations, in illusions, in hope, in fear, which binds men to each other, which binds together all humanity—the dead to the living and the living to the unborn.

It is only some such train of thought, or rather of feeling, that can in a measure explain the aim of the attempt, made in the tale which follows, to present an unrestful episode in the obscure lives of a few individuals out of all the disregarded multitude of the bewildered, the simple and the voiceless. For, if any part of truth dwells in the belief confessed above, it becomes evident that there is not a place of splendor or a dark corner of the earth that does not deserve, if only a passing glance of wonder and pity. The motive then, may be held to justify the matter of the work; but this preface, which is simply an avowal of endeavor, cannot end here-for the avowal is not yet complete.

Fiction—if it at all aspires to be art—appeals to temperament. And in truth it must be, like painting, like music, like all art, the appeal of one temperament to all the other innumerable temperaments whose subtle and resistless power endows passing events with their true meaning, and creates the moral, the emotional atmosphere of the place and time. Such an appeal to be effective must be an impression conveyed through the senses; and, in fact, it cannot be made in any other way, because temperament, whether individual or collective, is not amenable to persuasion. All art, therefore, appeals primarily to the senses, and the artistic aim when expressing itself in written words must also make its appeal through the senses, if its high desire is to reach the secret spring of responsive emotions. It must strenuously aspire to the plasticity of sculpture, to the color of painting, and to the magic suggestiveness of music-which is the art of arts. And it is only through complete, unswerving devotion to the perfect blending of form and substance; it is only through an unremitting never-discouraged care for the shape and ring of sentences that an approach can be made to plasticity, to color, and that the light of magic suggestiveness may be brought to play for an evanescent instant over the commonplace surface of words: of the old, old words, worn thin, defaced by ages of careless usage.

[…] My task which I am trying to achieve is, by the power of the written word, to make you hear, to make you feel-it is, before all, to make you see. That—and no more, and it is everything.

Unit 3　Setting and Theme: Herman Melville and his *Moby Dick*

3.1　Elements of Fiction: Setting and Theme

The overall **setting** of a narrative or dramatic work is the general locale, historical time, and social circumstances in which its action occurs. Setting falls into three categories: **the historical setting** refers to the approximate period of time during which a story takes place; **the geographical setting** refers to the actual location in which a story takes place including the physical features of a locale which help create a story's atmosphere; **the social setting** refers to the social conventions and the general environment by which characters may be constrained. Settings can be real or fictional, or a combination of both real and fictional elements. Most pieces of literature include more than one setting as the narrative progresses from place to place, shifts in time periods, moves in different social or cultural environments. Setting is an extremely important aspect of almost every piece of fiction. It can act almost as a nonhuman character affecting the characters in many different ways. Setting establishes the context of a story and sometimes the plot line of a story is so tied to its setting that it becomes the central factor in the meaning of a work. For example, in Fitzgerald *Great Gatsby,* the Jazz Age or the 1920s is the setting for the novel.

The **theme** in a story is its underlying message, or the central topic explored in a literary text. In other words, it is the "big idea" or the "main idea" the author tries to convey in a particular piece of writing. Themes are generally universal in nature, and related to the conditions of being human. Thus, the theme of literature transcends barriers of time, nation, and culture, as it concerns itself with the basic human experience and makes a story meaningful to people of any age, race or language. It is seldom stated explicitly, but rather expressed through the characters' actions, words, and thoughts.

3.2　Herman Melville and His Literary Life

Herman Melville (August 1, 1819—September 28, 1891) was an American novelist, short story writer, and poet of the American Renaissance period. His best-known works are *MobyDick* (1851); *Typee* (1846), a romanticized account of his experiences in Polynesia; *Billy Budd, Sailor*, a posthumously published novella. Although his reputation was not high at the time of his death, the 1919 centennial of his birth was the starting point of a Melville revival, and *Moby Dick* grew to be considered one of the great American novels.

Melville was born in New York City, the third child of a prosperous merchant whose death in 1832 left the family in dire financial straits. He took to sea in 1839 as a common sailor on a merchant ship and then on the whaler *Acushnet*, but he jumped ship in the Marquesas Islands. *Typee*, his first book, and its sequel, *Omoo* (1847), were travel-adventures based on his encounters with the peoples of the island. Their success gave him the financial security to marry Elizabeth Shaw, the daughter of the Boston jurist Lemuel Shaw. *Mardi* (1849), a romance-adventure and his first book, was not well received. *Redburn* (1849) and *White-Jacket* (1850), both tales based on his experience as a well-born young man at sea, were given respectable reviews, but did not sell well enough to support his expanding family.

Melville's growing literary ambition showed in *MobyDick* (1851), which took nearly a year and a half to write, but it did not find an audience, and critics scorned his psychological novel *Pierre: or, The Ambiguities* (1852). From 1853 to 1856, Melville published short fiction in magazines, including "Benito Cereno" and "Bartleby, the Scrivener". In 1857, he traveled to England, toured the Near East, and published his last work of prose, *The Confidence-Man* (1857). He moved to New York in 1863, eventually taking a position as United States customs inspector.

From that point, Melville focused his creative powers on poetry. *Battle-Pieces and Aspects of the War* (1866) was his poetic reflection on the moral questions of the American Civil War. In 1867, his eldest child Malcolm died at home from a self-inflicted gunshot. Melville's metaphysical epic *Clarel: A Poem and Pilgrimage in the Holy Land* was published in 1876. In 1886, his other son Stanwix died of apparent tuberculosis, and Melville retired. During his last years, he privately published two volumes of poetry, and left one volume unpublished. The novella *Billy Budd* was left unfinished at his death, but was published posthumously in 1924. Melville died from cardiovascular disease in 1891.

3.3　Introduction to *Moby Dick*

MobyDick; or, The Whale is an 1851 novel by Herman Melville. As a contribution to American Romanticism, *MobyDick* was published to mixed reviews: it was a commercial failure, and was out of print at the time of the author's death in 1891. Its reputation as a "Great American Novel" was established only in the 20th century, after the 1919 centennial of its author's birth. William Faulkner said he wished he had written the book himself, and D. H. Lawrence called it "one of the strangest and most wonderful books in the world" and "the greatest book of the sea ever written". In addition to a detailed account of the operations of the whaling industry, it is an encyclopedia of everything, history, philosophy, religion, and so on. But it is first a Shakespearean tragedy of man fighting against overwhelming odds in an indifferent and even hostile universe.

The story goes roughly as follows. Ishmael, feeling depressed, seeks escape by going out to sea on the whaling ship, Pequod. The captain is Ahab, the man with one leg. Moby Dick, the white whale, had sheared off his leg on a previous voyage, and Ahab resolves to hunt him to the kill. He hangs a doubloon on the mast as a reward for anyone who sights the whale first. The Pequod makes a good catch of whales but Ahab refuses to turn back until he has killed his enemy. Eventually the white whale appears, and the Pequod begins its doomed fight with it. On the first day the whale overturns a boat; on the second it swamps another. When the third day comes, Ahab and his crew manage to plunge a harpoon into it, but the whale carries the Pequod along with it to its doom. All on board the whalers get drowned, except one, Ishmael, who survives to tell the tale.

The **settings** of the novel are connected with the author's own experience and the whaling industry in that age.

Autobiographical elements. *MobyDick* draws on Melville's experience on the whaler "Acushnet". On December 30, 1840, Melville signed on as a green hand for the maiden voyage of the "Acushnet", planned to last for 52 months.

Whaling sources. In addition to his own experience on the whaling ship "Acushnet", two actual events served as the genesis for Melville's tale. One was the sinking of the Nantucket ship Essex in 1820, after a sperm whale rammed her 2,000 miles (3,200 km) from the western coast of South America. The other event was the alleged killing in the late 1830s of the albino sperm whale Mocha Dick, in the waters off the Chilean island of Mocha. Mocha Dick was rumored to have 20 or so harpoons in his back from other whalers, and appeared to attack ships with premeditated ferocity.

Several **themes** are revealed in *Moby Dick*. Alienation is sensed by Melville in his time on different levels, between man and man, man and society, and man and nature. Captain Ahab is a typical "isolator", who cuts himself off from his kids and wife, and stays away most of the time from his crew. He hates Moby Dick which is a symbol of nature. After the loss of his leg, he felt his pride is wounded by the white whale. He determines to avenge himself and hears of no objection. He becomes egocentric and loses his sanity and humanity, rushing towards his doom like a devilish creature. D.H. Lawrence remarks, "He (Melville) records also, almost beyond pain or pleasure, the extreme transitions of the isolated, far-driven soul, the soul which is now alone, without any real human contact."

The novel has also been read as a negative reflection upon American Transcendentalism, attacking the thought of leading Transcendentalist, Ralph Waldo Emerson in particular. The life and death of Ahab has been read as an attack on Emerson's philosophy of self-reliance, in its destructive potential and potential justification for egoism. Richard Chase writes that for Melville, "Death–spiritual, emotional, physical–is the price of self-reliance when it is pushed to the point of solipsism, where the world has no existence apart from the all-sufficient self."

In contemporary age, new theme can be read through this novel. It reflects the fighting between man and nature. The crew on Pequod, led by Ahab, symbolize human beings as a whole. The whale, Moby Dick, is the symbol of nature. Men, who violate the law of nature and dare to challenge it, are destined to be doomed, just like the fate of the crew in the novel. Moby Dick symbolizes the mysterious and overwhelming power of nature. It prepares to punish those who try to challenge its authority.

3.4 Selected Readings

CHAPTER 1. Loomings

Call me Ishmael. Some years ago—never mind how long precisely—having little or no money in my purse, and nothing particular to interest me on shore, I thought I would sail about a little and see the watery part of the world. It is a way I have of driving off the spleen and regulating the circulation. Whenever I find myself growing grim about the mouth; whenever it is a damp, drizzly November in my soul; whenever I find myself involuntarily pausing before coffin warehouses, and bringing up the rear of every funeral I meet; and especially whenever my hypos get such an upper hand of me, that it requires a strong moral principle to prevent me from deliberately stepping into the street, and methodically knocking people's hats off—then, I account it high time to get to sea as soon as I can. This is my substitute for pistol and ball. With a philosophical flourish Cato throws himself upon his sword; I quietly take to the ship. There is nothing surprising in this. If they but knew it, almost all men in their degree, some time or other, cherish very nearly the same feelings towards the ocean with me.

There now is your insular city of the Manhattoes, belted round by wharves as Indian isles by coral reefs—commerce surrounds it with her surf. Right and left, the streets take you waterward. Its extreme downtown is the battery, where that noble mole is washed by waves, and cooled by breezes, which a few hours previous were out of sight of land. Look at the crowds of water-gazers there.

Circumambulate the city of a dreamy Sabbath afternoon. Go from Corlears Hook to Coenties Slip, and from thence, by Whitehall, northward. What do you see?—Posted like silent sentinels all around the town, stand thousands upon thousands of mortal men fixed in ocean reveries. Some leaning against the spiles; some seated upon the pier-heads; some looking over the bulwarks of ships from China; some high aloft in the rigging, as if striving to get a still better seaward peep. But these are all landsmen; of week days pent up in lath and plaster—tied to counters, nailed to benches, clinched to desks. How then is this? Are the green fields gone? What do they here?

But look! Here come more crowds, pacing straight for the water, and seemingly bound for a dive. Strange! Nothing will content them but the extremist limit of the land; loitering under the shady lee of yonder warehouses will not suffice. No. They must get just as nigh the water as they possibly can without falling in. And there they stand—miles of them—leagues. Inlanders all, they come from lanes and alleys, streets and avenues—north, east, south, and west. Yet here they all unite. Tell me, does the magnetic virtue of the needles of the compasses of all those ships attract them thither?

Once more. Say you are in the country; in some high land of lakes. Take almost any path you please, and ten to one it carries you down in a dale, and leaves you there by a pool in the stream. There is magic in it. Let the most absent-minded of men be plunged in his deepest reveries—stand that man on his legs, set his feet a-going, and he will infallibly lead you to water, if water there be in all that region. Should you ever be athirst in the great American desert, try this experiment, if your caravan happen to be supplied with a metaphysical professor. Yes, as every one knows, meditation and water are wedded for ever.

But here is an artist. He desires to paint you the dreamiest, shadiest, quietest, most enchanting bit of romantic landscape in all the valley of the Saco. What is the chief element he employs? There stand his trees, each with a hollow trunk, as if a hermit and a crucifix were within; and here sleeps his meadow, and there sleep his cattle; and up from yonder cottage goes a sleepy smoke. Deep into distant woodlands winds a mazy way, reaching to overlapping spurs of mountains bathed in their hill-side blue. But though the picture lies thus tranced, and though this pine-tree shakes down its sighs like leaves upon this shepherd's head, yet all were vain, unless the shepherd's eye were fixed upon the magic stream before him. Go visit the Prairies in June, when for scores on scores of miles you wade knee-deep among Tiger-lilies—what is the one charm wanting?—Water—there is not a drop of water there! Were Niagara but a cataract of sand, would you travel your thousand miles to see it? Why did the poor poet of Tennessee, upon suddenly receiving two handfuls of silver, deliberate whether to buy him a coat, which he sadly needed, or invest his money in a pedestrian trip to Rockaway Beach? Why is almost every robust healthy boy with a robust healthy soul in him, at some time or other crazy to go to sea? Why upon your first voyage as a passenger, did you yourself feel such a mystical vibration, when first told that you and your ship were now out of sight of land? Why did the old Persians hold the sea holy? Why did the Greeks give it a separate deity, and own brother of Jove? Surely all this is not without meaning. And still deeper the meaning of that story of Narcissus, who because he could not grasp the tormenting, mild image he saw in the fountain, plunged into it and was drowned. But that same image, we ourselves see in all rivers and oceans. It is the image of the ungraspable phantom of life; and this is the key to it all.

Now, when I say that I am in the habit of going to sea whenever I begin to grow hazy about the eyes, and begin to be over conscious of my lungs, I do not mean to have it inferred that I ever go to sea as a passenger. For to go as a passenger you must needs have a purse, and a purse is but a rag unless you have something in it. Besides, passengers get sea-sick—grow quarrelsome—don't sleep of nights—do not enjoy themselves much, as a general thing;—no, I never go as a passenger; nor, though I am something of a salt, do I ever go to sea as a Commodore, or a Captain, or a Cook. I abandon the glory and distinction of such offices to those who like them. For my part, I abominate all honorable respectable toils, trials, and tribulations of every kind whatsoever. It is quite as much as I can do to take care of myself, without taking care of ships, barques, brigs, schooners, and what not. And as for going as cook,—though I confess there is considerable glory in that, a cook being a sort of officer on ship-board—yet, somehow, I never fancied broiling fowls;—though once broiled, judiciously buttered, and judgmatically salted and peppered, there is no one who will speak more respectfully, not to say reverentially, of a broiled fowl than I will. It is out of the idolatrous dotings of the old Egyptians upon broiled ibis and roasted river horse, that you see the mummies of those creatures in their huge bake-houses the pyramids.

No, when I go to sea, I go as a simple sailor, right before the mast, plumb down into the forecastle, aloft there to the royal mast-head. True, they rather order me about some, and make me jump from spar to spar, like a grasshopper in a May meadow. And at first, this sort of thing is unpleasant enough. It touches one's sense of honor, particularly if you come of an old established family in the land, the Van Rensselaers, or Randolphs, or Hardicanutes. And more than all, if just previous to putting your hand into the tar-pot, you have been lording it as a country schoolmaster, making the tallest boys stand in awe of you. The transition is a keen one, I assure you, from a schoolmaster to a sailor, and requires a strong decoction of Seneca and the Stoics to enable you to grin and bear it. But even this wears off in time.

What of it, if some old hunks of a sea-captain orders me to get a broom and sweep down the decks? What does that indignity amount to, weighed, I mean, in the scales of the New Testament? Do you think the archangel Gabriel thinks anything the less of me, because I promptly and respectfully obey that old hunks in that particular instance? Who ain't a slave? Tell me that. Well, then, however the old sea-captains may order me about—however they may thump and punch me about, I have the satisfaction of knowing that it is all right; that everybody else is one way or other served in much the same way—either in a physical or metaphysical point of view, that is; and so the universal thump is passed round, and all hands should rub each other's shoulder-blades, and be content.

Again, I always go to sea as a sailor, because they make a point of paying me for my trouble, whereas they never pay passengers a single penny that I ever heard of. On the contrary, passengers themselves must pay. And there is all the difference in the world between paying and being paid. The act of paying is perhaps the most uncomfortable infliction that the two orchard thieves entailed upon us. But *being paid*,—what will compare with it? The urbane activity with which a man receives money is really marvelous, considering that we so earnestly believe money to be the root of all earthly ills, and that on no account can a monied man enter heaven. Ah! How cheerfully we consign ourselves to perdition!

Finally, I always go to sea as a sailor, because of the wholesome exercise and pure air of the fore-castle deck. For as in this world, head winds are far more prevalent than winds from astern (that is, if you never violate the Pythagorean maxim), so for the most part the Commodore on the quarter-deck gets his atmosphere at second hand from the sailors on the forecastle. He thinks he breathes it first; but not so. In much the same way do the commonalities lead their leaders in many other things, at the same time that the leaders little suspect it. But wherefore it was that after having repeatedly smelt the sea as a merchant sailor, I should now take it into my head to go on a whaling voyage; this the invisible police officer of the Fates, who has the constant surveillance of me, and secretly dogs me, and influences me in some unaccountable way—he can better answer than any one else. And, doubtless, my going on this whaling voyage, formed part of the grand programme of Providence that was drawn up a long time ago. It came in as a sort of brief interlude and solo between more extensive performances. I take it that this part of the bill must have run something like this:

"*Grand Contested Election for the Presidency of the United States.*" "WHALING VOYAGE BY ONE ISHMAEL." "BLOODY BATTLE IN AFFGHANISTAN."

Though I cannot tell why it was exactly that those stage managers, the Fates, put me down for this shabby part of a whaling voyage, when others were set down for magnificent parts in high tragedies, and short and easy parts in genteel comedies, and jolly parts in farces—though I cannot tell why this was exactly; yet, now that I recall all the circumstances, I think I can see a little into the springs and motives which being cunningly presented to me under various disguises, induced me to set about performing the part I did, besides cajoling me into the delusion that it was a choice resulting from my own unbiased freewill and discriminating judgment.

Chief among these motives was the overwhelming idea of the great whale himself. Such a portentous and mysterious monster roused all my curiosity. Then the wild and distant seas where he rolled his island bulk; the undeliverable, nameless perils of the whale; these, with all the attending marvels of a thousand Patagonian sights and sounds, helped to sway me to my wish. With other men, perhaps, such things would not have been inducements; but as for me, I am tormented with an everlasting itch for things remote. I love to sail forbidden seas, and land on barbarous coasts. Not ignoring what is good, I am quick to perceive a horror, and could still be social with it—would they let me—since it is but well to be on friendly terms with all the inmates of the place one lodges in.

By reason of these things, then, the whaling voyage was welcome; the great flood-gates of the wonder-world swung open, and in the wild conceits that swayed me to my purpose, two and two there floated into my inmost soul, endless processions of the whale, and, mid most of them all, one grand hooded phantom, like a snow hill in the air.

Questions for discussion:

1. Why does Ishmael choose to go to the sea? What kind of work does he do on the sea?
2. Why does Ishmael mention the story of Narcissus?
3. What is the point of view in this selected reading?

3.5　Appreciation of Selected Readings

《白鲸》（*Moby Dick*）由美国作家赫曼·梅尔维尔创作于 1851 年，被视为美国最伟大的长篇小说之一。书中的白鲸事实上是一头白色的抹香鲸，船长艾哈布（Ahab）在远航出海的时候遇到了这头白色的鲸鱼，与之展开恶战，被咬掉了一条腿。艾哈布船长恼羞成怒，发誓要为自己复仇，他搜遍大洋上的每个地方，甚至不惜牺牲船上所有水手的性命，最终与白鲸同归于尽。船上的唯一的幸存者以什梅尔（Ishmael）作为故事的叙述者，向读者们讲述了故事的前因后果。

《白鲸》这本书在梅尔维尔生前并没有引起世人的关注，尤其是艾哈布船长这个形象的塑造，与同时代以爱默生为代表的超验主义者所倡导的"自立者"（self-reliance）形象是冲突的。艾哈布船长是一个典型的超验主义自立者，在受到白鲸的攻击后，不惜一切代价为自己复仇，一个以自我为中心的人物，最终酿成了悲剧，是一个典型的唯我论（solipsism）分子。

艾哈布悲剧的根源在于对大自然力量的错误认知。书中的白鲸是大自然力量的象征。艾哈布试图打败白鲸以挽回自己的骄傲，事实上就是与大自然的神秘力量对抗。在原始社会时期，人类对于未知的大自然怀有深深的恐惧，用丰富的想象力塑造了神的世界。当人类进入工业社会，随着人类对自然的不断探索以及受到资本主义人文主义思想的影响，以自我为中心、崇尚人的力量的人类把自己视为大自然的主人，不断地向大自然索取，企图征服它。艾哈布的故事就是一个妄图征服自然的典型。人类社会进入到 20 世纪 60 年代，美国作家蕾切尔·卡逊在《寂静的春天》一书中描写了因过度使用化学药品和肥料而导致的环境污染和生态破坏最终给人类带来的灾难。他指出人类以破坏生态环境为代价获取的发展无异于饮鸩止渴。从艾哈布的悲剧我们可以看到，人类与自然之间不能简单地理解为征服与被征服的关系，二者之间相互依存，只有遵循自然的规律，才能实现人与自然之间的和谐共存。

3.6　Supplementary Reading

Science and Civilization (1932)

by Aldous Huxley

Our civilization, as each one of us is uncomfortably aware, is passing through a time of crisis. Why should this be? What are the causes of our present troubles. Most of them are due, in the last resort, to the fact that science has been applied to human affairs, but not applied adequately or consistently. In the past man's worst enemy was Nature. He lived under the continual threat of famine and pestilence; a wet summer could bring death to whole nations, and every winter was a menace. Mountains stood like a barrier between people and people; a sea was less a highway than an impassable division. Today Nature, though still an enemy, is an enemy almost completely conquered. Modern agriculture assures us of an ample food supply. Modern transportation has made the resources of the entire planet accessible to all its inhabitants. Modern medicine and sanitation allow dense populations to cover the ground without risk of pestilence. True, we are still at the mercy of the more violent natural convulsions. Against earthquake, flood, and hurricane man has, as yet, devised no adequate protection. But these major cataclysms are rare. At most times Nature is no longer formidable; she has been subdued.

Our present troubles are not, then, due to Nature: they are entirely artificial, genuinely home-made. The very arts and sciences which we have used to conquer Nature have turned on their creators and are now conquering us. The present economic disasters are of our own making; we have brought them on ourselves by allowing our mechanical and agricultural science to develop more rapidly than our economic science. We cannot buy what we produce, and are therefore compelled to keep our factories idle and let our fields lie fallow. Millions are hungry, but wheat has to be thrown into the sea. This is where, at the moment, science has brought us.

[...]

Everyone admits in principle that human activities must be regulated scientifically; but when it comes to applying this principle, two questions arise. Science, in the present context, is a means to an end—but what end? That is the first question. And (this is the second question) by whom is this instrument to be used? Who is to wield the power which science gives?

Many definitions of the ideal human society have been attempted. That which, I suppose, the majority of modern men and women would find most acceptable is what, for want of a better name, I will call the "humanistic" definition. The humanist is one who believes that our human nature can and should be developed harmoniously as a whole—that the sacrifices which man must always make should be made in his own highest interest, and not in the interest of something external to himself—not in the name of any less or any more than human cause. For the humanist, then, the ideal society is one whose constituent members are all physically, intellectually, and morally of the best quality; a society so organized that no individual shall be unjustly treated or compelled to waste or bury his talents; a society which gives its members the greatest possible amount of individual liberty, but at the same time provides them with the most satisfying incentives to altruistic effort; a society not static but deliberately progressive, consciously tending towards the realization of the highest human aspirations. Science might be made a means for the creation of such a society, but only on certain conditions: that the powers which science confers must be used by rulers who are fundamentally humanist.

Our present crisis is mainly and most obviously economic. The fact is dangerous; for it means that the ends pursued by our rulers, at any rate in the immediate future, will be primarily economic ends. It means that the instrument of science will be used by men primarily interested in economics, and only secondarily, if at all, in the higher humanistic values.

[…]

I will add a few more words by way of summary and epilogue. Science in itself is morally neutral; it becomes good or evil according as it is applied. Ideally, science should be applied by humanists. In this case it would be good. In actual fact, it is more likely to be applied by economists, and so to turn out, if not wholly bad, at any rate a very mixed blessing. It rests with us and our descendants to decide whether we shall use the unprecedented power which science gives us for good or for bad purposes. It is in our hands to choose wisely or unwisely. Alas, that wisdom should be so much harder to come by than knowledge!

Unit 4　Characters and Characterization: William Somerset Maugham and his *The Moon and Six Pence*

4.1　Elements of Fiction: Characters and Characterization

Characters are the persons represented in a dramatic or narrative works, who are interpreted by the reader as being endowed with particular moral, intellectual, and emotional qualities by inferences from what the persons say and their distinctive ways of saying it—the dialogue, and from what they do—the action. A character may remain essentially "stable", or unchanged in the outlook or disposition, from beginning to the end of a work, which is assumed as **flat character**. A character may undergo radical change, either through a gradual process of development, or as the result of a crisis, which is considered to be a **round character**.

In *Aspects of the Novel*, E.M. Forster illustrated the distinction between flat and round characters. A flat character is built around "a single idea or quality" and is presented without much individualizing detail, and therefore can be fairly adequately described in a single phrase or sentence. A round character is complex in temperament and motivation, and is presented in subtle particularity; such a character therefore is as difficult to describe with any adequacy as a person in real life.

The main character was formerly referred to as **hero or heroine**, but a more neutral term **protagonist** has taken their place in literary works, because, under certain circumstance, the main character in more recent fiction is not the heroic type, but is rather an anti-hero, one who is ill equipped to cope with the situation. On the opposite end stands the antagonist, the major character in a narrative or drama that works against the protagonist.

Characterization, the process of creating imaginary characters, is a crucial part of making a story compelling. Authors achieve this by providing details that make characters individual and particular. Good characterization gives readers a strong sense of characters' personalities and complexities and it makes characters vivid, alive and believable. There are two fundamental ways of characterization in fiction, the direct method and indirect method, someone labels them to be telling and showing.

Characterization can be direct, as when an author tells the reader what the characters are like. In telling, the author intervenes authoritatively in order to describe, and often to evaluate, the motives and dispositional qualities of the characters. For example, in Jane Austen's *Pride and Prejudice* (1813), Jane described Mr. Bennet as follows:

Mr. Bennet was so odd a mixture of quick parts, sarcastic humour, reserve, and caprice, that the experience of three-and-twenty years had been insufficient to make his wife understand his character.

Characterization can also be indirect, as when an author shows the readers what the characters are like. In showing, the author simply presents the characters talking and acting and leaves the readers to infer the motives and dispositions that lie behind what they say and do. The author may show not only external speech and action, but also a character's inner thoughts, feelings, and responsiveness to events, which is typically represented by stream of consciousness.

4.2 William Somerset Maugham and His Literary Life

William Somerset Maugham (1874—1965) was born in Paris when his father was a solicitor at the British Embassy there, and he received his early education in France. But both his mother and father died during his childhood respectively when he was eight and ten years old, and he went to live in England under the rigorous care of his uncle, an awesome clergyman. He led a rather unhappy life both in his uncle's home and at the King's School. He studied philosophy for a short period at Heidelberg University in Germany and there he first cultivated his lasting interest in drama and painting, but his early years in France and his extensive reading in French literature in his short childhood sojourn in southern France had much influence upon his literary taste and style. He refused to be ordained as a clergyman and took up the study of medicine and surgery. He was qualified as a doctor but never practiced medicine. He travelled extensively on the European Continent, particularly in Italy and Spain, then settled down for a number of years in Paris and moved among painters and writers there. All this acquaintance with foreign lands was largely responsible for his adoption of a writer's career, for the cosmopolitanism and broad perspective in his writings, and also for his employment of Paul Ganguin's life and career in his novel *The Moon and Sixpence*.

Maugham started writing novels in the late 1890s, but his first novel based on his hospital experience of the miseries of the slum patients, *Liza of Lambeth* (1897), was completely neglected upon its appearance. In the first decade of the 20th century he turned to the writing of plays and quite unexpectedly popular success came to him as a playwright when in 1908 four of his plays (*Lady Frederick, Jack Straw, Mrs. Dot and The Explorer*) ran successfully at the same time in the West End theaters in London (creating an almost unprecedented success story in London theatrical history) and were subsequently popular also on the American stage. From then on till the early thirties Maugham became an established dramatist and wrote upwards of altogether thirty plays, but he also took time off to write novels and short stories and other prose writings, especially his most important, semi-autobiographical novel *Of Human Bondage* (1915).

Throughout his life, Maugham traveled a lot and he had much of his experience told in his collections of short stories and novels. In this chapter, his *The Moon and Sixpence* will be discussed, focusing on its characters and characterization.

4.3   Introduction to *The Moon and Sixpence*

The Moon and Sixpence is a novel by W. Somerset Maugham, first published on 15 April 1919. Maugham tells the story in episodic form in the first person singular, himself serving as a participant in the story as well as the narrator. The story is, in part, based on the life of the painter Paul Gauguin. The three parts of Charles Strickland's career, in London, in Paris, and in Tahiti are retold by the author with himself as an eye-witness or as a researcher, in order to add to the vividness of the story.

Strickland was a well-off, middle-class stockbroker in London, sometime in the late 19th or early 20th century. Early in the novel, he left his wife and children and went to Paris. He lived a destitute but defiantly content life there as a painter, lodging in run-down hotels and falling prey to both illness and hunger. Motivated by his drive for art, Strickland cared nothing for physical discomfort and was indifferent to his surroundings. He was helped and supported by a commercially successful but hackneyed Dutch painter, Dirk Stroeve, coincidentally, who recognized Strickland's genius as a painter. After helping Strickland recover from a life-threatening illness, Stroeve was repaid by having his wife, Blanche, abandon him for Strickland. Strickland later discarded the wife, because all he really wanted from Blanche was to be a model to paint, not serious companionship. It was hinted in the novel that he indicated that to her, but she took the risk anyway. Blanche then committed suicide. She was another human casualty in Strickland's single-minded pursuit of art and beauty, the first casualties being his own established life, and those of his wife and children.

After the Paris episode, the story continued in Tahiti. Strickland had already died, and the narrator attempted to piece together his life there from recollections of others. He found that Strickland had taken up with a native woman, had two children by her (one of whom died), and started painting profusely. The narrator learned that Strickland had settled for a short while in the French port of Marseilles before traveling to Tahiti, where he lived for a few years before dying of leprosy. Strickland left behind numerous paintings, but his magnum opus, which he painted on the walls of his hut before losing his sight to leprosy, was burnt by his wife after his death, which was assumed to be his dying order.

Characters are the persons represented in a dramatic or narrative works, who are interpreted by readers as being endowed with particular moral, intellectual, and emotional qualities by inferences from what the persons say and their distinctive ways of saying it. As the **protagonist** in *The Moon and Sixpence,* while in London, Charles Strickland appears very seldom in person but is known and described chiefly as the dull, uninteresting stockbroker husband of Mrs. Strickland, who is a vivacious lady interested in arts and a friend to the author. Only the sudden disastrous disappearance of Strickland and its exasperating consequence upon his wife are given prominence in the narrative. Charles Strickland figures large in the author's numerous encounters with him in Paris, where he goes to fulfill his ruling passion of becoming a painter. The hero is as repulsive as ever, in fact even more so than before, but the author stresses above all the man's uncontrollable desire to paint so that all other common pleasures in life seem unimportant to him and he becomes even extremely unreasonable in his dealings with others, including his wife and children, and his friends ready to help him.

Throughout the story, Charles Strickland develops from a rigid stockbroker to a fanatic pursuer for art, from a traditional husband and father to an irresponsible man who bites the hand that feeds him. He is a **round character** with complex personalities. In order to increase the authenticity of the story, the author acts as a narrator and participant in the story. He is an acquaintance of Strickland's wife and even witnesses some important stages in Strickland's life. The author creates Strickland in a direct way. He tells and comments the deeds by Strickland. Through his narration, a selfish and unprincipled man with fanatic pursuit for art is presented before readers.

4.4   Selected Readings

Chapter XIV

During the journey back to England I thought much of Strickland. I tried to set in order what I had to tell his wife. It was unsatisfactory, and I could not imagine that she would be content with me; I was not content with myself. Strickland perplexed me. I could not understand his motives. When I had asked him what first gave him the idea of being a painter, he was unable or unwilling to tell me. I could make nothing of it. I tried to persuade myself than an obscure feeling of revolt had been gradually coming to a head in his slow mind, but to challenge this was the undoubted fact that he had never shown any impatience with the monotony of his life. If, seized by an intolerable boredom, he had determined to be a painter merely to break with irksome ties, it would have been comprehensible, and commonplace; but commonplace is precisely what I felt he was not. At last, because I was romantic, I devised an explanation which I acknowledged to be far-fetched, but which was the only one that in any way satisfied me. It was this: I asked myself whether there was not in his soul some deep-rooted instinct of creation, which the circumstances of his life had obscured, but which grew relentlessly, as a cancer may grow in the living tissues, till at last it took possession of his whole being and forced him irresistibly to action. The cuckoo lays its egg in the strange bird's nest, and when the young one is hatched it shoulders its foster-brothers out and breaks at last the nest that has sheltered it.

But how strange it was that the creative instinct should seize upon this dull stockbroker, to his own ruin, perhaps, and to the misfortune of such as were dependent on him; and yet no stranger than the way in which the spirit of God has seized men, powerful and rich, pursuing them with stubborn vigilance till at last, conquered, they have abandoned the joy of the world and the love of women for the painful austerities of the cloister. Conversion may come under many shapes, and it may be brought about in many ways. With some men it needs a cataclysm, as a stone may be broken to fragments by the fury of a torrent; but with some it comes gradually, as a stone may be worn away by the ceaseless fall of a drop of water. Strickland had the directness of the fanatic and the ferocity of the apostle.

But to my practical mind it remained to be seen whether the passion which obsessed him would be justified of its works. When I asked him what his brother-students at the night classes he had attended in London thought of his painting, he answered with a grin:

"They thought it a joke."

"Have you begun to go to a studio here?"

"Yes. The blighter came round this morning—the master, you know; when he saw my drawing he just raised his eyebrows and walked on."

Strickland chuckled. He did not seem discouraged. He was independent of the opinion of his fellows.

And it was just that which had most disconcerted me in my dealings with him. When people say they do not care what others think of them, for the most part they deceive themselves. Generally they mean only that they will do as they choose, in the confidence that no one will know their vagaries; and at the utmost only that they are willing to act contrary to the opinion of the majority because they are supported by the approval of their neighbours. It is not difficult to be unconventional in the eyes of the world when your unconventionality is but the convention of your set. It affords you then an inordinate amount of self-esteem. You have the self-satisfaction of courage without the inconvenience of danger. But the desire for approbation is perhaps the most deeply seated instinct of civilised man. No one runs so hurriedly to the cover of respectability as the unconventional woman who has exposed herself to the slings and arrows of outraged propriety. I do not believe the people who tell me they do not care a row of pins for the opinion of their fellows. It is the bravado of ignorance. They mean only that they do not fear reproaches for peccadillos which they are convinced none will discover.

But here was a man who sincerely did not mind what people thought of him, and so convention had no hold on him; he was like a wrestler whose body is oiled; you could not get a grip on him; it gave him a freedom which was an outrage. I remember saying to him:

"Look here, if everyone acted like you, the world couldn't go on."

"That's a damned silly thing to say. Everyone doesn't want to act like me. The great majority are perfectly content to do the ordinary thing."

And once I sought to be satirical.

"You evidently don't believe in the maxim: Act so that every one of your actions is capable of being made into a universal rule."

"I never heard it before, but it's rotten nonsense."

"Well, it was Kant who said it."

"I don't care; it's rotten nonsense."

Nor with such a man could you expect the appeal to conscience to be effective. You might as well ask for a reflection without a mirror. I take it that conscience is the guardian in the individual of the rules which the community has evolved for its own preservation. It is the policeman in all our hearts, set there to watch that we do not break its laws. It is the spy seated in the central stronghold of the ego. Man's desire for the approval of his fellows is so strong, his dread of their censure so violent, that he himself has brought his enemy within his gates; and it keeps watch over him, vigilant always in the interests of its master to crush any half-formed desire to break away from the herd. It will force him to place the good of society before his own. It is the very strong link that attaches the individual to the whole. And man, subservient to interests he has persuaded himself are greater than his own, makes himself a slave to his taskmaster. He sits him in a seat of honour. At last, like a courtier fawning on the royal stick that is laid about his shoulders, he prides himself on the sensitiveness of his conscience. Then he has no words hard enough for the man who does not recognise its sway; for, a member of society now, he realises accurately enough that against him he is powerless. When I saw that Strickland was really indifferent to the blame his conduct must excite, I could only draw back in horror as from a monster of hardly human shape.

The last words he said to me when I bade him good-night were:

"Tell Amy it's no good coming after me. Anyhow, I shall change my hotel, so she wouldn't be able to find me."

"My own impression is that she's well rid of you." I said.

"My dear fellow, I only hope you'll be able to make her see it. But women are very unintelligent."

Questions for discussion:

1.　What's the narrator's comment about Strickland's desire of being a painter?

2.　Do you care other people's approval for your deeds?

3.　If you are confronted with the conflict between ideals and reality, how will you solve it?

4.　Some says *The Moon and Sixpence* is influenced by aestheticism, do you agree?

4.5　Appreciation of Selected Readings

《月亮与六便士》（*The Moon and Sixpence*）是英国作家毛姆的长篇小说，成书于 1919 年。小说以法国印象派画家保罗·高更（Paul Gauguin）的生平为素材，讲述了一位平凡的伦敦证券经纪人，斯特里克兰，出于对艺术的狂热，在忍受了长达 17 年的平凡家庭生活后，抛妻弃子，逃离在他人看来优裕美满的生活，奔赴南太平洋的塔希提岛，用画笔谱写光辉灿烂的艺术人生。

"六便士"是当时英国最小的货币单位。毛姆的一位朋友开玩笑说，人们仰望月亮时，往往忘记了踩在脚下的六便士。月亮寓意理想，而六便士象征现实生活。毛姆在小说中探寻了现实与理想之间的矛盾，但是并没有真正找到解决二者之间矛盾的方法。作品主人公采用了当时西方社会盛行的逃避现实的方法以追求内心的安宁。

在斯特里克兰的一生中，有三位女性贯穿了他的一生，第一位是斯特里克兰太太，她为斯特里克兰养育了一对儿女；第二位是画家施特略夫的妻子勃朗什，她因照顾斯特里克兰并在充当其模特的过程中爱上了他，在遭受抛弃后自杀；第三位是塔希提岛上的土著女子爱塔，她勤劳、善良、质朴的情感和物质条件满足了斯特里克兰内心对宁静生活的向往以及安心创作的物质保障。当理想与现实冲突时，斯特里克兰毫不顾忌道德责任的束缚，抛妻弃子，只为填补内心的狂热追求；而勃朗什对他而言仅仅只有看护和模特的作用，当自己康复并完成画作之后，随即被弃如敝屣；爱塔的物质条件可以保证其创作时衣食无忧，而在他患上麻风病去世后，还嘱咐爱塔将房子和画作付之一炬，丝毫不考虑爱塔和孩子以后的生活。

读者可以把斯特里克兰视为一个行动派——人到中年，恐惧内心不断褪色的理想，毅然抛弃一切去追寻心中的"月亮"。理想的实现却是建立在对他人伤害的基础之上。斯特里克兰是自私的，他是一个背弃了社会道德约束、家庭责任担当的人，行事作风属于典型的利己主义者。当理性与现实冲突时，他没有理性思考，而是采取了逃避现实的做法。故事虽然取材于高更的生平，却塑造了一个超出现实生活的人物，小说以斯特里克兰与他的作品同时消失而结尾，将故事中的是与非交由读者来评判。

4.6　Supplementary Reading

The Rocking-Horse Winner

by D.H. Lawrence

There was a woman who was beautiful, who started with all the advantages, yet she had no luck. She married for love, and the love turned to dust. She had bonny children, yet she felt they had been thrust upon her, and she could not love them. They looked at her coldly, as if they were finding fault with her. And hurriedly she felt she must cover up some fault in herself. Yet what it was that she must cover up she never knew. Nevertheless, when her children were present, she always felt the center of her heart go hard. This troubled her, and in her manner she was all the more gentle and anxious for her children, as if she loved them very much. Only she herself knew that at the center of her heart was a hard little place that could not feel love, no, not for anybody. Everybody else said of her: "She is such a good mother. She adores her children." Only she herself, and her children themselves, knew it was not so. They read it in each other's eyes.

There were a boy and two little girls. They lived in a pleasant house, with a garden, and they had discreet servants, and felt themselves superior to anyone in the neighborhood.

Although they lived in style, they felt always an anxiety in the house. There was never enough money. The mother had a small income, and the father had a small income, but not nearly enough for the social position which they had to keep up. The father went in to town to some office. But though he had good prospects, these prospects never materialized. There was always the grinding sense of the shortage of money, though the style was always kept up.

At last the mother said: "I will see if I can't make something." But she did not know where to begin. She racked her brains, and tried this thing and the other, but could not find anything successful. The failure made deep lines come into her face. Her children were growing up, they would have to go to school. There must be more money, there must be more money. The father, who was always very handsome and expensive in his tastes, seemed as if he never would be able to do anything worth doing. And the mother, who had a great belief in herself, did not succeed any better, and her tastes were just as expensive.

And so the house came to be haunted by the unspoken phrase: There must be more money! There must be more money! The children could hear it all the time, though nobody said it aloud. They heard it at Christmas, when the expensive and splendid toys filled the nursery. Behind the shining modern rocking-horse, behind the smart doll's house, a voice would start whispering: "There must be more money! There must be more money!" And the children would stop playing, to listen for a moment. They would look into each other's eyes, to see if they had all heard. And each one saw in the eyes of the other two that they too had heard. "There must be more money! There must be more money!"

It came whispering from the springs of the still-swaying rocking-horse, and even the horse, bending his wooden, champing head, heard it. The big doll, sitting so pink and smirking in her new pram, could hear it quite plainly, and seemed to be smirking all the more self-consciously because of it. The foolish puppy, too, that took the place of the teddy-bear, he was looking so extraordinarily foolish for no other reason but that he heard the secret whisper all over the house: "There must be more money!"

Yet nobody ever said it aloud. The whisper was everywhere, and therefore no one spoke it. Just as no one ever says: "We are breathing!" in spite of the fact that breath is coming and going all the time.

"Mother," said the boy Paul one day, "why don't we keep a car of our own? Why do we always use uncle's, or else a taxi?"

"Because we're the poor members of the family," said the mother.

"But why are we, mother?"

"Well—I suppose," she said slowly and bitterly, "it's because your father has no luck."

The boy was silent for some time.

"Is luck money, mother?" he asked rather timidly.

"No, Paul. Not quite. It's what causes you to have money."

"Oh!" said Paul vaguely. "I thought when Uncle Oscar said filthy lucker, it meant money."

"Filthy Lucre does mean money," said the mother. "But it's lucre, not luck."

"Oh!" said Paul vaguely. "Then what is luck, mother?"

"It's what causes you to have money. If you're lucky you have money. That's why it's better to be born lucky than rich. If you're rich, you may lose your money. But if you're lucky, you will always get more money."

"Oh! Will you? And is father not lucky?"

"Very unlucky, I should say," she said bitterly.

The boy watched her with unsure eyes.

"Why?" he asked.

"I don't know. Nobody ever know why one person is lucky and another unlucky."

"Don't they? Nobody at all? Does nobody know?"

"Perhaps God. But He never tells."

"He ought to, then. And aren't you lucky either, mother?"

"I can't be, if I married an unlucky husband."

"But by yourself, aren't you?"

"I used to think I was, before I married. Now I think I am very unlucky indeed."

"Why?"

"Well—never mind! Perhaps I'm not really," she said.

The child looked at her, to see if she meant it. But he saw, by the lines of her mouth, that she was only trying to hide something from him.

"Well, anyhow," he said stoutly, "I'm a lucky person."

"Why?" said his mother, with a sudden laugh.

He stared at her. He didn't even know why he had said it.

"God told me," he asserted, brazening it out.

"I hope He did, dear!" she said, again with a laugh, but rather bitter.

"He did, mother!"

"Excellent!" said the mother, using one of her husband's exclamations.

The boy saw she did not believe him; or, rather, that she paid no attention to his assertion. This angered him somewhat, and made him want to compel her attention.

He went off by himself, vaguely, in a childish way, seeking for the clue to "luck." Absorbed, taking no heed of other people, he went about with a sort of stealth, seeking inwardly for luck. He wanted luck, he wanted it, he wanted it. When the two girls were playing dolls in the nursery, he would sit on his big rocking-horse, charging madly into space, with a frenzy that made the little girls peer at him uneasily. Wildly the horse careered the waving dark hair of the boy tossed, his eyes had a strange glare in them. The little girls dared not speak to him.

When he had ridden to the end of his made little journey, he climbed down and stood in front of his rocking-horse, staring fixedly into its lowered face. Its red mouth was slightly open, its big eye was wide and glassy-bright.

"Now!" he would silently command the snorting steed. "Now, take me to where there is luck! Now take me!"

And he would slash the horse on the neck with the little whip he had asked Uncle Oscar for. He knew the horse could take him to where there was luck, if only he forced it. So he would mount again, and start on his furious ride, hoping at last to get there. He knew he could get there.

"You'll break your horse, Paul!" said the nurse.

"He's always riding like that! I wish he'd leave off!" said his elder sister Joan.

But he only glared down on them in silence. Nurse gave him up. She could make nothing of him. Anyhow he was growing beyond her.

One day his mother and his Uncle Oscar came in when he was on one of his furious rides. He did not speak to them.

"Hallo, you young jockey! Riding a winner?" said his uncle.

"Aren't you growing too big for a rocking-horse? You're not a very little boy any longer, you know," said his mother.

But Paul only gave a blue glare from his big, rather close-set eyes. He would speak to nobody when he was in full tilt. His mother watched him with an anxious expression on her face.

At last he suddenly stopped forcing his horse into the mechanical gallop, and slid down.

"Well, I got there!" he announced fiercely, his blue eyes still flaring, and his sturdy long legs straddling apart.

"Where did you get to?" asked his mother.

"Where I wanted to go," he flared back at her.

"That's right, son!" said Uncle Oscar. "Don't you stop till you get there. What's the horse's name?"

"He doesn't have a name," said the boy.

"Gets on without all right?" asked the uncle.

"Well, he has different names. He was called Sansovino last week."

"Sansovino, eh? Won the Ascot . How did you know his name?"

"He always talks about horse-races with Bassett," said Joan.

The uncle was delighted to find that his small nephew was posted with all the racing news. Bassett, the young gardener, who had been wounded in the left foot in the war and had got his present job through Oscar Cresswell whose batman he had been was a perfect blade of the "turf". He lived in the racing events, and the small boy lived with him.

Oscar Cresswell got it all from Bassett.

"Master Paul comes and asks me, so I can't do more than tell him, sir," said Bassett, his face terribly serious, as if he were speaking of religious matters.

"And does he ever put anything on a horse he fancies?"

"Well—I don't want to give him away—he's a young sport, a fine sport, sir. Would you mind asking him himself? He sort of takes a pleasure in it, and perhaps he'd feel I was giving him away, sir, if you don't mind."

Bassett was serious as a church.

The uncle went back to his nephew and took him off for a ride in the car.

"Say, Paul, old man, do you ever put anything on a horse?" the uncle asked.

The boy watched the handsome man closely.

"Why, do you think I oughtn't to?" he parried.

"Not a bit of it. I thought perhaps you might give me a tip for the Lincoln."

The car sped on into the country, going down to Uncle Oscar's place in Hampshire.

"Honor bright?" said the nephew.

"Honor bright, son!" said the uncle.

"Well, then, Daffodil."

"Daffodil! I doubt it, sonny. What about Mirza?"

"I only know the winner," said the boy. "That's Daffodil."

"Daffodil, eh?"

There was a pause. Daffodil was an obscure horse comparatively.

"Uncle!"

"Yes, son?"

"You won't let it go any further, will you? I promised Bassett."

"Bassett be damned, old man! What's he got to do with it?"

"We're partners. We've been partners from the first. Uncle, he lent me my first five shillings, which I lost, I promised him, honor bright, it was only between me and him; only you gave me that ten-shilling note I started winning with, so I thought you were lucky. You won't let it go any further, will you?"

The boy gazed at his uncle from those big, hot, blue eyes, set rather close together. The uncle stirred and laughed uneasily.

"Right you are, son! I'll keep your tip private. Daffodil, eh? How much are you putting on him?"

"All except twenty pounds," said the boy. "I keep that in reserve."

The uncle thought it a good joke.

"You keep twenty pounds in reserve, do you, you young romancer? What are you betting, then?"

"I'm betting three hundred," said the boy gravely. "But it's between you and me, Uncle Oscar! Honor bright?"

The uncle burst into a roar of laughter.

"It's between you and me all right, you young Nat Gould," he said, laughing. "But where's your three hundred?"

"Bassett keeps it for me. We're partners."

"You are, are you! And what is Bassett putting on Daffodil?"

"He won't go quite as high as I do, I expect. Perhaps he'll go a hundred and fifty."

"What, pennies?" laughed the uncle.

"Pounds," said the child, with a surprised look at his uncle. "Bassett keeps a bigger reserve than I do."

Between wonder and amusement Uncle Oscar was silent. He pursued the matter no further, but he determined to take his nephew with him to the Lincoln races.

"Now, son," he said, "I'm putting twenty on Mirza, and I'll put five for you on any horse you fancy. What's your pick?"

"Daffodil, uncle."

"No, not the fiver on Daffodil!"

"I should if it was my own fiver," said the child.

"Good! Good! Right you are! A fiver for me and a fiver for you on Daffodil."

The child had never been to a race-meeting before, and his eyes were blue fire. He pursed his mouth tight, and watched. A Frenchman just in front had put his money on Lancelot. Wild with excitement, he flayed his arms up and down, yelling, "Lancelot! Lancelot!" in his French accent.

Daffodil came in first, Lancelot second, Mirza third. The child flushed and with eyes blazing, was curiously serene. His uncle brought him four five-pound notes, fourto one.

"What am I to do with these?" he cried, waving them before the boy's eyes.

"I suppose we'll talk to Bassett," said the boy. "I expect I have fifteen hundred now; and twenty in reserve; and this twenty."

His uncle studied him for some moments.

"Look here, son!" he said. "You're not serious about Bassett and that fifteen hundred, are you?"

"Yes, I am. But it's between you and me, uncle. Honor bright!"

"Honor bright all bright, son! But I must talk to Bassett."

"If you'd like to be a partner, uncle, with Bassett and me, we could all be partners. Only, you'd have to promise, honor bright, uncle, not to let it go beyond us three. Bassett and I are lucky, and you must be lucky, because it was your ten shillings. I started winning with…."

Uncle Oscar took both Bassett and Paul into Richmond Park for an afternoon, and there they talked.

"It's like this, you see, sir," Bassett said. "Master Paul would get me talking about racing events, spinning yearns, you know, sir. And he was always keen on knowing if I'd made or if I'd lost. It's about a year since, now, that I put five shillings on Blush of Dawn for him--and we lost. Then the luck turned, with that ten shillings, he had from you, that we put on Singhalese. And since that time, it's been pretty steady, all things considering. What do you say, Master Paul?"

"We're all right when we're sure," said Paul. "It's when we're not quite sure that we go down."

"Oh, but we're careful then," said Bassett.

"But when are you sure?" smiled Uncle Oscar.

"It's Master Paul, sir," said Bassett, in a secret, religious voice. "It's as if he had it from heaven. Like daffodil, now, for the Lincoln. That was as sure as eggs."

"Did you put anything on Daffodil?" asked Oscar Cresswell.

"Yes, sir. I made my bid."

"And my nephew?"

Bassett was obstinately silent, looking at Paul.

"I made twelve hundred, didn't I, Bassett? I told uncle I was putting three hundred on Daffodil."

"That's right," said Bassett, nodding.

"But where's the money?" asked the uncle.

"I keep it safe locked up, sir. Master Paul he can have it any minute he likes to ask for it."

"What, fifteen hundred pounds?"

"And twenty! And forty, that is, with the twenty he made on the course."

"It's amazing!" said the uncle.

"If Master Paul offers you to be partners, sir, I would if I were you; if you'll excuse me," said Bassett.

Oscar Cresswell thought about it.

"I'll see the money," he said.

They drove home again, and sure enough, Bassett came round to the garden-house with fifteen hundred pounds in notes. The twenty pounds reserve was left with Joe Glee in the Turf Commission deposit.

"You see, it's all right, uncle, when I'm sure! Then we go strong, for all we're worth. Don't we, Bassett?"

"We do that, Master Paul."

"And when are you sure?" said the uncle, laughing.

"Oh, well, sometimes I'm absolutely sure, like about Daffodil," said the boy; "and sometimes I have an idea; and sometimes I haven't even an idea, have I, Bassett? Then we're careful, because we mostly go down."

"You do, do you! And when you're sure, like about Daffodil, what makes you sure, sonny?"

"Oh, well, I don't know," said the boy uneasily. "I'm sure, you know, uncle; that's all."

"It's as if he had it from heaven, sir," Bassett reiterated.

"I should say so!" said the uncle.

But he became a partner. And when he Leger was coming on Paul was "sure" about Lively Spark, which was a quite inconsiderable horse. The boy insisted on putting a thousand on the horse, Bassett went for five hundred, and Oscar Cresswell two hundred. Lively Spark came in first, and the betting had been ten to one against him. Paul had made ten thousand.

"You see," he said, "I was absolutely sure of him."

Even Oscar Cresswell had cleared two thousand.

"Look here, son," he said, "this sort of thing makes me nervous."

"It needn't, uncle! Perhaps I shan't be sure again for a long time."

"But what are you going to do with your money?" asked the uncle.

"Of course," said the boy, "I started it for mother. She said she had no luck, because father is unlucky, so I thought if I was lucky, it might stop whispering."

"What might stop whispering?"

"Our house. I hate our house for whispering."

"What does it whisper?"

"Why-why"-the boy fidgeted- "why, I don't know. But it's always short of money, you know, uncle."

"I know it, son, I know it."

"You know people send mother writs, don't you, uncle?"

"I'm afraid I do," said the uncle.

"And then the house whispers, like people laughing at you behind your back. It's awful, that is! I thought if I was lucky…"

"You might stop it," added the uncle.

The boy watched him with big blue eyes, that had an uncanny cold fire in them, and he said never a word.

"Well, then!" said the uncle. "What are we doing?"

"I shouldn't like mother to know I was lucky," said the boy.

"Why not, son?"

"She'd stop me."

"I don't think she would."

"Oh!"—and the boy writhed in and odd way— "I don't want her to know, uncle."

"All right, son! We'll manage it without her knowing."

They managed it very easily. Paul, at the other's suggestion, handed over five thousand pounds to his uncle, who deposited it with the family lawyer, who was then to inform Paul's mother that a relative had put five thousand pounds into his hands, which sum was to be paid out a thousand pounds at a time, on the mother's birthday, for the next five years.

"So she'll have a birthday present of a thousand pounds for five successive years," said Uncle Oscar. "I hope it won't make it all the harder for her later."

Paul's mother had her birthday in November. The house had been "whispering" worse than ever lately, and, even in spite of his luck, Paul could not bear up against it. He was very anxious to see the effect of the birthday letter, telling his mother about the thousand pounds.

When there was no visitors, Paul now took his meals with his parents, as he was beyond the nursery control. His mother went into town nearly every day. She had discovered that she had an odd knack of sketching furs and dress materials, so she worked secretly in the studio of a friend who was the chief "artist" for the leading drapers. She drew the figures of ladies in furs and ladies in silk and sequins for the newspaper advertisements. This young woman artist earned several thousand pounds a year, but Paul's mother only made several hundreds, and she was again dissatisfied. She so wanted to be first in something, and she did not succeed, even in making sketches for drapery advertisements.

She was down to breakfast on the morning of her birthday. Paul watched her face as she read her letters. He knew the lawyer's letter. As his mother read it, her face hardened and became more expressionless. Then a cold, determined look came on her mouth. She hid the letter under the pile of others, and said not a word about it.

"Didn't you have anything nice in the post for your birthday, mother?" said Paul.

"Quite moderately nice," she said, her voice cold and absent.

She went away to town without saying more.

But in the afternoon Uncle Oscar appeared. He said Paul's mother had had a long interview with the lawyer, asking if the whole five thousand could not be advanced at once, as she was in debt.

"What do you think, uncle?" said the boy.

"I leave it to you, son."

"Oh, let her have it, then! We can get some more with the other," said the boy.

"A bird in the hand is worth two in the bush, laddie!" said Uncle Oscar.

"But I'm sure to know for the Grand National; or the Lincolnshire; or else the Derby. I'm sure to know for one of them," said Paul.

So Uncle Oscar signed the agreement, and Paul's mother touched the whole five thousand. Then something very curious happened. The voices in the house suddenly went mad, like a chorus of frogs on a spring evening. There were certain new furnishings, and Paul had a tutor. He was really going to Eton, his father's school, in the following autumn. There were flowers in the winter, and a blossoming of the luxury Paul's mother had been used to. And yet the voices in the house, behind the sprays of mimosa and almond blossom, and from under the piles of iridescent cushions, simply trilled and screamed in a sort of ecstasy: "There must be more money! Oh-h-h; there must be more money. Oh, now, now-w! Now-w-w-there must be more money! -more than ever! More than ever!"

It frightened Paul terribly. He studied away at his Latin and Greek with his tutors. But his intense hours were spent with Bassett. The Grand National had bone by: he had not "known", and had lost a hundred pounds. Summer was at hand. He was in agony for the Lincoln. But even for the Lincoln he didn't "know", and he lost fifty pounds. He became wild-eyed and strange, as if something were going to explode in him.

"Let it alone, son! Don't you bother about it!" urged Uncle Oscar. But it was as if the boy couldn't really hear what his uncle was saying.

"I've got to know for the Derby! I've got to know for the Derby!" the child reiterated, his big blue eyes blazing with a sort of madness.

His mother noticed how overwrought he was.

"You'd better go to the seaside. Wouldn't you like to go now to the seaside, instead of waiting? I think you'd better," she said, looking down at him anxiously, her heart curiously heavy about him.

But the child lifted his uncanny blue eyes.

"I couldn't possibly go before the derby, mother!" he said. "I couldn't possibly!"

"Why not?" she said, her voice becoming heavy when she was opposed. "Why not? You can still go from the seaside to see the Derby with your Uncle Oscar, if that's what you wish. No need for you to wait here. Besides, I think you care too much about these races. It's a bad sign. My family has been a gambling family, and you won't know till you grow up how much damage it has done. But it has done damage. I shall have to send Bassett away, and ask Uncle Oscar not to talk racing to you, unless you promise to be reasonable about it; go away to the seaside and forget it. You're all nerves!"

"I'll do what you like, mother, so long as you don't send me away till after the Derby," the boy said.

"Send you away from where? Just from this house?"

"Yes," he said, gazing at her.

"Why, you curious child, what makes you care about this house so much, suddenly? I never knew you loved it."

He gazed at her without speaking. He had a secret within a secret, something he had not divulged, even to Bassett or to his Uncle Oscar.

But his mother, after standing undecided and a little bit sullen for some moments, said:

"Very well, then! Don't go to the seaside till after the Derby, if you don't wish it. But promise me you won't let your nerves to go pieces. Promise you won't think so much about horse-racing and events, as you call them."

"Oh, no," said the boy casually. "I won't think much about them, mother. You needn't worry. I wouldn't worry, mother, if I were you."

"If you were me and I were you," said his mother, "I wonder what we should do!"

"But you know you needn't worry, mother, don't you?" the boy repeated.

"I should be awfully glad to know it," she said wearily.

"Oh, well, you can, you know. I mean, you ought to know you needn't worry," he insisted.

"Ought I? Then I'll see about it," she said.

Paul's secret of secrets was his wooden horse, that which had no name. Since he was emancipated from a nurse and a nursery-governess, he had had his rocking-horse removed to his own bedroom at the top of the house.

"Surely, you're too big for a rocking-horse!" his mother had remonstrated.

"Well, you see, mother, till I can have a real horse, I like to have some sort of animal about," had been his quaint answer.

"Do you feel he keeps you company?" she laughed.

"Oh, yes! He's very good, he always keeps me company, when I'm there," said Paul.

So the horse, rather shabby, stood in an arrested prance in the boy's bedroom.

The Derby was drawing near, and the boy grew more and more tense. He hardly heard what was spoken to him, he was very frail, and his eyes were really uncanny. His mother had sudden strange seizures of uneasiness about him. Sometimes, for half-an-hour, she would feel a sudden anxiety about him that was almost anguish. She wanted to rush to him at once, and know he was safe.

Two nights before the Derby, she was at a big party in town, when one of her rushes of anxiety about her boy, her first-born, gripped her heart till she could hardly speak. She fought with the feeling, might and main, for she believed in common-sense. But it was too strong. She had to leave the dance and go downstairs to telephone to the country. The children's nursery-governess was terribly surprised and startled at being rung up in the night.

"Are all the children all right, Miss Wilmot?"

"Oh, yes, they are quite all right."

"Master Paul? Is he all right?"

"He went to bed as right as a trivet . Shall I run up and look at him?"

"No," said Paul's mother reluctantly. "No! Don't trouble. It's all right. Don't sit up. We shall be home fairly soon." She did not want her son's privacy intruded upon.

"Very good," said the governess.

It was about one o'clock when Paul's mother and father drove up to their house. All was still. Paul's mother went to her room and slipped off her white fur cloak. She had told her maid not to wait up for her. she heard her husband downstairs, mixing a whisky-and-soda.

And then, because of the strange anxiety at her heart, she stole upstairs to her son's room. Noiselessly she went along the upper corridor. Was there a faint noise? What was it?

She stood, with arrested muscles, outside his door, listening. There was a strange, heavy, and yet not loud noise. Her heart stood still. It was a soundless noise, yet rushing and powerful. Something huge, in violent, hushed motion. What was it? What in God's name was it? She ought to know. She felt that she knew the noise. She knew what it was.

Yet she could not place it. She couldn't say what it was. And on and on it went, like a madness.

Softly, frozen with anxiety and fear, she turned the door-handle.

The room was dark. Yet in the space near the window, she heard and saw something plunging to and fro. She gazed in fear and amazement.

Then suddenly she switched on the light, and saw her son, in his green pajamas, madly surging on the rocking-horse. The blaze of light suddenly lit him up, as he urged the wooden horse, and lit her up, as she stood, blonde, in her dress of pale green and crystal, in the doorway.

"Paul!" she cried. "Whatever are you doing?"

"It's Malabar!" he screamed, in a powerful, strange voice. "It's Malabar!"

His eyes blazed at her for one strange and senseless second, as he ceased urging his wooden horse. Then he fell with a crash to the ground, and she, all her tormented motherhood flooding upon her, rushed to gather him up.

But he was unconscious, and unconscious he remained, with some brain-fever. He talked and tossed, and his mother sat stonily by his side.

"Malabar! It's Malabar! Bassett, Bassett, I know! It's Malabar!"

So the child cried, trying to get up and urge the rocking-horse that gave him his inspiration.

"What does he mean by Malabar?" asked the heart-frozen mother.

"I don't know," said the father stonily.

"What does he mean by Malabar?" she asked her brother Oscar.

"It's one of the horses running for the Derby," was the answer.

And, in spite of herself, Oscar Cresswell spoke to Bassett, and himself put a thousand on Malabar: at fourteen to one.

The third day of the illness was critical: they were waiting for a change. The boy, with his rather long, curly hair, was tossing ceaselessly on the pillow. He neither slept nor regained consciousness, and his eyes were like blue stones. His mother sat, feeling her heart had gone, turned actually into a stone.

In the evening, Oscar Cresswell did not come, but Bassett sent a message, saying could he come up for one moment, just one moment? Paul's mother was very angry at the intrusion, but on second thought she agreed. The boy was the same. Perhaps Bassett might bring him to consciousness.

The gardener, a shortish fellow with a little brown moustache, and sharp little brown eyes, tiptoed into the room touched his imaginary cap to Paul's mother, and stole to the bedside, staring with glittering, smallish eyes, at the tossing, dying child.

"Master Paul!" he whispered. "Master Paul! Malabar came in first all right, a clean win. I did as you told me. You've made over seventy thousand pounds, you have; you've got over eight thousand. Malabar came in all right, Master Paul."

"Malabar! Malabar! Did I say Malabar, mother? Did I say Malabar? Do you think I'm lucky, mother? I knew Malabar, didn't I? Over eighty thousand pounds! I call that lucky, don't you, mother? Over eighty thousand pounds! I knew, didn't I know I knew? Malabar came in all right. If I ride my horse till I'm sure, then I tell you, Bassett, you can go as high as you like. Did you go for all you were worth, Bassett?"

"I went a thousand on it, Master Paul."

"I never told you, mother, that if I can ride my horse, and get there, then I'm absolutely sure—oh, absolutely! Mother, did I ever tell you? I am lucky!"

"No, you never did," said the mother.

But the boy died in the night.

And even as he lay dead, his mother heard her brother's voice saying to her: "My God, Hester, you're eighty-odd thousand to the good, and a poor devil of a son to the bad. But, poor devil, poor devil, he's best gone out of a life where he rides his rocking-horse to find a winner."

Unit 5   Narrator and Point of View: Alice Walker's *Everyday Use for Your Grandmama*

5.1   Elements of Fiction: Narrator and Point of View

Every story is told or narrated by someone, and the narrator of a story is of great importance. The narrator determines the story's point of view and the implications of this are far-reaching. For instance, the author may tell the same story from the perspective of mother, father, daughter, or neighbour. Each of them may give a different story, depending on who tells it. The narrator is not the same as the author, even the author uses "I" as the narrative voice. Sometimes, an author will employ an unreliable narrator, one who will not tell the truth, or the whole truth. The narrator could be biased or so the facts might be partially selected or unfairly judged. Such bias and partiality of the unreliable narrator need to be put right by the reader in the process of reading.

Point of view signifies the way a story gets told-the mode (or modes) established by an author by means of which the reader is presented with the characters, dialogue, actions, setting and events which constitute the narrative in a work of a fiction. Authors have developed many different ways to present a story, and many single works exhibit a diversity of methods. The most widely used modes are first-person narration and third-person narration.

In a **first-person narrative**, the narrator speaks as "I", and is to a greater or lesser degree a participant in the story. This mode limits the matter of the narrative to what the first-person narrator knows, experiences, infers, or can find out: by talking to other characters. We distinguish between the narrative "I" who is only a fortuitous witness and auditor of the matters he relates; or who is a participant, but only a minor or peripheral one; or who is himself or herself the central character in the story.

In a **third-person narrative**, the narrator is someone outside the story proper who refers to all the characters in the story by name, or as "he", "she", "they". The third-person narrative can be divided into the omniscient point view and limited point of view. In an **omniscient third-person perspective**, the narrator knows everything that needs to be known about the agents, actions, and events, and has privileged access to the characters' thoughts, feelings, and motives; also, the narrator is free to move at will in time and place, to shift from character to character, and to report (or conceal) their speech, doings and states of consciousness. In a **limited third-person perspective**, the narrator stays inside the confines of what is perceived, thought, remembered and felt by single character (or at most by very few characters) within the story. The limited point of view is frequently applied in stream-of-consciousness narration.

In the second-person point of view, the story gets told solely, or at least primarily, as an address by the narrator to someone he calls by the second-person pronoun "you". Authors rarely adopt this narrative mode.

5.2　Alice Walker and Her Literary Life

As an important African America novelist of contemporary period, Alice Walker (1944-) was born into a sharecropper's family in Eatonton, Georgia. She attended Spelman College in Atalanta, Georgia, and finished her education in Sarah Lawrence College in Bronxville, New York. She began writing in college and published her first works—poems as well as stories in 1965. Later she received fellowships in support of her writing career. She has, by virtue of the great amount of fiction, poetry, and essays she has written over the years, made herself a central figure in contemporary American literature. In addition to her volumes of poetry and short stories, she has published quite a few novels such as *The Third Life of Grange Copeland* (1970), *Meridian* (1976), *The Color Purple* (1982), *The Temple of My Familiar* (1989), and *Possessing the Secret of Joy* (1990). Her greatest achievement so far is her novel, *The Color Purple*, which won for her both the American Book Award and the Pulitzer Prize.

5.3　Introduction to *Everyday Use for Your Grandmama*

Everyday Use for Your Grandmama is a short story by Alice Walker. It was first published in the April 1973 issue of *Harper's Magazine* and is part of Walker's short story collection *In Love and Trouble*. It has since become widely studied and frequently anthologized. Four characters are involved in the short story:

Dee: She is an educated African-American woman and the elder daughter of Mrs. Johnson. She wants to obtain her cultural identity through changing her name from Dee to Wangero Leewanikhia Kemanjo (an African name). She marries a Muslim man, and acquires artifacts from Mama's house to put on display, an approach that puts her at odds with Mama and Maggie. She is physically beautiful and is described as having a great sense of style.

Mrs. Johnson: She is described as a "large, big-boned woman with rough, man-working hands." She enjoys her lifestyle (especially milking cows) and did not receive an education past second grade. She is against Dee's way of living, but says nothing about it in order to respect her and stay civil.

Maggie: Mrs. Johnson describes her as dull and much more brittle and quieter compared to her older sister. She is Mama's younger daughter, who has burn scars and marks from the burning down of their prior home and she is very nervous and self-conscious because of it. She leads a simple and traditional life with her mother in the South. She has very limited reading ability.

Hakim-a-barber: Dee's partner who is referred to as "Asalamalakim" (a Muslim greeting). He tells Mama to call him "Hakim-a-barber" due to Mama being unable to pronounce his real name.

The story unfolds through the eyes and opinions of Mama. Mama is the **narrator**, and the **POV** of it is in the first-person narration. As Maggie and Mama wait for Dee to arrive for a visit, Mama's mind wanders with various thoughts and memories of Dee, giving the audience an impartial view of Dee as being self-centered and uncaring. Due to the fact that readers are getting only one viewpoint, it is uncertain if Dee truly does exhibit these characteristics or if it is only Mama's opinion of the eldest daughter that is being forced upon us. It is thought by some that Mama does not judge her children, Dee and Maggie, accurately due to Mama's own insecurities. This is evidenced during Mama's daydream of Dee and herself on an imaginary popular talk show under the context of children who have "made it". Mama notes being overweight and rough around the edges and refers to the fact that Dee is ashamed of Mama's appearance. As Mama continues to narrate the story, the audience continues to get a sense of Dee's snobbish personality, along with moments of doubt as readers see glimpses of Mama's own shortcomings. As the story concludes, the audience is left with the vision of Mama and Maggie remaining alone on the front lawn basking in the simplicity of each other and the straightforward life that has been built.

In the story, Mama acts as an unreliable narrator and her ideas about Dee are of personal impartiality. Readers should judge by themselves while reading.

5.4 Selected Readings

Everyday Use for Your Grandmama

I will wait for her in the yard that Maggie and I made so clean and wavy yesterday afternoon. A yard like this is more comfortable than most people know. It is not just a yard. It is like an extended living room. When the hard clay is swept clean as a floor and the fine sand around the edges lined with tiny, irregular grooves, anyone can come and sit and look up into the elm tree and wait for the breezes that never come inside the house.

Maggie will be nervous until after her sister goes: she will stand hopelessly in corners, homely and ashamed of the burn scars down her arms and legs, eying her sister with a mixture of envy and awe. She thinks her sister has held life always in the palm of one hand, that "no" is a word the world never learned to say to her.

You've no doubt seen those TV shows where the child who has "**made it**"[1] is confronted, as a surprise, by her own mother and father, tottering in weakly from backstage. (A Pleasant surprise, of course: What would they do if parent and child came on the show only to curse out and insult each other?) On TV mother and child embrace and smile into each other's face. Sometimes the mother and father weep, the child wraps them in her arms and leans across the table to tell how she would not have made it without their help. I have seen these programs.

Sometimes I dream a dream in which Dee and I are suddenly brought together on a TV program of this sort. Out of dark and soft-seated limousine I am ushered into a bright room filled with many people. There I meet a smiling, gray, sporty man like **Johnny Carson**[2] who shakes my hand and tells me what a fine girl I have. Then we are on the stage and Dee is embracing me with tears in her eyes. She pins on my dress a large orchid, even though she has told me once that she thinks or chides are tacky flowers.

In real life I am a large, big-boned woman with rough, man-working hands. In the winter I wear flannel nightgown to bed and overalls during the day. I can kill and clean a hog as mercilessly as a man. My fat keeps me hot in zero weather. I can work outside all day, breaking ice to get water for washing; I can eat pork liver cooked over the open tire minutes after it comes steaming from the hog. One winter I knocked a bull calf straight in the brain between the eyes with a sledge hammer and had the meat hung up to chill be-fore nightfall. But of course all this does not show on television. I am the way my daughter would want me to be: a hundred pounds lighter, my skin like an uncooked barley pancake. My hair glistens in the hot bright lights. Johnny Carson has much to do to keep up with my quick and witty tongue.

But that is a mistake. I know even before I wake up. Who ever knew a Johnson with a quick tongue? Who can even imagine me looking a strange white man in the eye? It seems to me I have talked to them always with one toot raised in flight, with my head turned in whichever way is farthest from them. Dee, though. She would always look anyone in the eye. Hesitation was no part of her nature.

"How do I look, Mama?" Maggie says, showing just enough of her thin body enveloped in pink skirt and red blouse for me to know she's there, almost hidden by the door.

"Come out into the yard," I say.

Have you ever seen a lame animal, perhaps a dog run over by some careless person rich enough to own a car, sidle up to someone who is ignorant enough to be kind of him? That is the way my Maggie walks. She has been like this, chin on chest, eyes on ground, feet in shuffle, ever since the fire that burned the other house to the ground.

Dee is lighter than Maggie, with nicer hair and a fuller figure. She's a woman now, though sometimes I forget. How long ago was it that the other house burned? Ten, twelve years? Sometimes I can still hear the flames and feel Maggie's arms sticking to me, her hair smoking and her dress falling off her in little black papery flakes. Her eyes seemed stretched open, blazed open by the flames reflected in them. And Dee. I see her standing off under the sweet gum tree she used to dig gum out of; a look at concentration on her face as she watched the last dingy gray board of the house tall in toward the red-hot brick chimney. Why don't you do a dance around the ashes? I'd wanted to ask her. She had hated the house that much.

I used to think she hated Maggie, too. But that was before we raised the money, the church and me, to send her to Augusta to school. She used to read to us without pity, forcing words, lies, other folks' habits, whole lives upon us two, sitting trapped and ignorant underneath her voice. She washed us in a river of make-believe, burned us with a lot of knowledge we didn't necessarily need to know. Pressed us to her with the serious way she read, to shove us away at just the moment, like dimwit we seemed about to understand.

Dee wanted nice things. A yellow organdy dress to wear to her graduation from high school; black pumps to match a green suit she'd made from an old suit somebody gave me. She was determined to stare down any disaster in her efforts. Her eyelids would not flicker for minutes at a time. Often I fought off the temptation to shake her. At sixteen she had a style of her own' and knew what style was.

I never had an education myself. After second grade the school was closed down.

Don't ask me why. in 1927 colored asked fewer questions than they do now. Sometimes Maggie reads to me. She stumbles along good-naturedly but can't see well. She knows she is not bright. Like good looks and money, quickness passed her by. She will marry John Thomas (who has mossy teeth in an earnest face) and then I'll be free to sit here and I guess just sing church songs to myself. Although I never was a good singer. Never could carry a tune. I was always better at a man's job. 1 used to love to milk till I was **hooked**[3] in the side in '49. Cows are soothing and slow and don't bother you, unless you try to milk them the wrong way.

I have deliberately turned my back on the house. It is three rooms, just like the one that burned, except the roof is tin: they don't make shingle roofs any more. There are no real windows, just some holes cut in the sides, like the portholes in a ship, but not round and not square, with rawhide holding the shutter s up on the outside. This house is in a pasture, too, like the other one. No doubt when Dee sees it she will want to tear it down. She wrote me once that no matter where we "choose" to live, she will manage to come see us. But she will never bring her friends. Maggie and I thought about this and Maggie asked me, Mama, when did Dee ever have any friends?"

She had a few. Furtive boys in pink shirts hanging about on washday after school. Nervous girls who never laughed. Impressed with her they worshiped the well-turned phrase, the cute shape, the scalding humor that erupted like bubbles in lye. She read to them.

When she was courting **Jimmy T**[4] she didn't have much time to pay to us, but turned all her faultfinding power on him. He flew to marry a cheap city girl from a family of ignorant flashy people. She hardly had time to recompose herself.

When she comes I will meet—but there they are!

Maggie attempts to make a dash for the house, in her shuffling way, but I stay her with my hand. "Come back here," I say. And she stops and tries to dig a well in the sand with her toe.

It is hard to see them clearly through the strong sun. But even the first glimpse of leg out of the car tells me it is Dee. Her feet were always neat-looking, as it God himself had shaped them with a certain style. From the other side of the car comes a short, stocky man. Hair is all over his head a foot long and hanging from his chin like a kinky mule tail. I hear Maggie suck in her breath. "Uhnnnh," is what it sounds like.

Like when you see the wriggling end of a snake just in front of your toot on the road. "Uhnnnh."

Dee next. A dress down to the ground, in this hot weather. A dress so loud it hurts my eyes. There are yellows and oranges enough to throw back the light of the sun. I feel my whole face warming from the heat waves it throws out. Earrings gold, too, and hanging down to her shoulders. Bracelets dangling and making noises when she moves her arm up to shake the folds of the dress out of her armpits. The dress is loose and flows, and as she walks closer, I like it. I hear Maggie go "Uhnnnh" again. It is her sister's hair. It stands straight up like the wool on a sheep. It is black as night and around the edges are two long pigtails that rope about like small lizards disappearing behind her ears.

"**Wa-su-zo-Tean-o!**"[5] she says, coming on in that gliding way the dress makes her move. The short stocky fellow with the hair to his navel is all grinning and he follows up with "**Asalamalakim**[6], my mother and sister!" He moves to hug Maggie but she falls back, right up against the back of my chair. I feel her trembling there and when I look up I see the perspiration falling off her chin.

"Don't get up," says Dee. Since I am stout it takes something of a push. You can see me trying to move a second or two before I make it. She turns, showing white heels through her sandals, and goes back to the car. Out she peeks next with a **Polaroid**[7]. She stoops down quickly and lines up picture after picture of me sitting there in front of the house with Maggie cowering behind me. She never takes a shot without making sure the house is included. When a cow comes nibbling around the edge of the yard she snaps it and me and Maggie and the house. Then she puts the Polaroid in the back seat of the car, and comes up and kisses me on the forehead.

Meanwhile Asalamalakim is going through motions with Maggie's hand. Maggie's hand is as limp as a fish, and probably as cold, despite the sweat, and she keeps trying to pull it back. It looks like Asalamalakim wants to shake hands but wants to do it fancy. Or maybe he don't know how people shake hands. Anyhow, he soon gives up on Maggie.

"Well," I say. "Dee."

"No, Mama," she says. "Not 'Dee', Wangero Leewanika Kemanjo!"

"What happened to 'Dee'?" I wanted to know.

"She's dead," Wangero said. "I couldn't bear it any longer, being named after the people who oppress me."

"You know as well as me you was named after your aunt Dicle," I said. Dicie is my sister. She named Dee. We called her "Big Dee" after Dee was born.

"But who was she named after?" asked Wangero.

"I guess after Grandma Dee," I said.

"And who was she named after?" asked Wangero.

"Her mother," I said, and saw Wangero was getting tired. "That's about as far back as I can trace it," I said.

Though, in fact, I probably could have carried it back beyond the **Civil War**[8] through the **branches**[9].

"Well," said Asalamalakim, "there you are."

"Uhnnnh," I heard Maggie say.

"There I was not," I said, before 'Dicie' cropped up in our family, so why should I try to trace it that far back?"

He just stood there grinning, looking down on me like somebody inspecting a Model A car. Every once in a while he and Wangero sent eye signals over my head.

"How do you pronounce this name?" I asked.

"You don't have to call me by it if you don't want to," said Wangero.

"Why shouldn't I?" I asked. "If that's what you want us to call you, we'll call you. "

"I know it might sound awkward at first," said Wangero.

"I'll get used to it," I said. "**Ream it out again**[10]."

Well, soon we got the name out of the way. Asalamalakim had a name twice as long and three times as hard. After I tripped over it two or three times he told me to just call him Hakim-a-barber. I wanted to ask him was he a barber, but I didn't really think he was, so I don't ask.

"You must belong to those beet-cattle peoples down the road," I said. They said "Asalamalakim" when they met you too, but they didn't Shake hands. Always too busy feeding the cattle, fixing the fences, putting up salt-lick shelters, throwing down hay. When the white folks poisoned some of the herd the men stayed up all night with rifles in their hands. I walked a mile and a half just to see the sight.

Hakim-a-barber said, "I accept some of their doctrines, but farming and raising cattle is not my style." (They didn't tell me, and I didn't ask, whether Wangero (Dee) had really gone and married him.)

We sat down to eat and right away he said he didn't eat collards and pork was unclean. Wangero, though, went on through the **chitlins**[11] and corn bread, the greens and everything else. She talked a blue streak over the sweet potatoes. Everything delighted her. Even the fact that we still used the benches her daddy made for the table when we couldn't afford to buy chairs.

"Oh, Mama!" she cried. Then turned to Hakim-a-barber. "I never knew how lovely these benches are. You can feel the **rump prints**[12]," she said, running her hands underneath her and along the bench. Then she gave a sigh and her hand closed over Grandma Dee's butter dish. "That's it!" she said. "I knew there was something I wanted to ask you if I could have." She jumped up from the table and went over in the corner where the churn stood, the milk in it clabber by now. She looked at the churn and looked at it.

"This churn top is what I need," she said. "Didn't Uncle Buddy whittle it out of a tree you all used to have?"

"Yes," I said.

"Uh huh, " she said happily. "And I want the dasher, too."

"Uncle Buddy whittle that, too?" asked the barber.

Dee (Wangero) looked up at me.

"Aunt Dee's first husband whittled the dash," said Maggie so low you almost couldn't hear her. "His name was Henry, but they called him Stash."

"Maggie's brain is like an elephant," Wangero said, laughing. "I can use the churn top as a center piece for the alcove table," she said, sliding a plate over the churn, "and I'll think of something artistic to do with the dasher."

When she finished wrapping the dasher the handle stuck out. I took it for a moment in my hands. You didn't even have to look close to see where hands pushing the dasher up and down to make butter had left a kind of **sink**[13] in the wood. In fact, there were a lot of small sinks; you could see where thumbs and fingers had sunk into the wood. It was beautiful light yellow wood, from a tree that grew in the yard where Big Dee and Stash had lived.

After dinner Dee (Wangero) went to the trunk at the foot of my bed and started rifling through it. Maggie hung back in the kitchen over the dishpan. Out came Wangero with two quilts. They had been pieced by Grandma Dee and then Big Dee and me had hung them on the quilt frames on the front porch and quilted them. One was in the Lone Star pattern. The other was Walk Around the Mountain. In both of them were scraps of dresses Grandma Dee had worn fifty and more years ago. Bit sand pieces of Grandpa Jarrell's Paisley shirts. And one teeny faded blue piece, about the size of a penny matchbox, that was from Great Grandpa Ezra's uniform that he wore in the Civil War.

"Mama," Wangero said sweet as a bird. "Can I have these old quilts?"

I heard something fall in the kitchen, and a minute later the kitchen door slammed.

"Why don't you take one or two of the others?" 1 asked. "These old things was just done by me and Big Dee from some tops your grandma pieced before she died."

"No," said Wangero. "I don't want those. They are stitched around the borders by machine."

"That'll make them last better," I said.

"That's not the point," said Wanglero. "These are all pieces of dresses Grandma used to wear. She did all this stitching by hand. Imagine!" She held the quilts securely in her arms, stroking them.

"Some of the pieces, like those lavender ones, come from old clothes her mother handed down to her," I said, moving up to touch the quilts. Dee (Wangero) moved back just enough so that I couldn't reach the quilts. They already belonged to her. "Imagine!" she breathed again, clutching them closely to her bosom.

"The truth is," I said, "I promised to give them quilts to Maggie, for when she marries John Thomas."

She gasped like a bee had stung her.

"Maggie can't appreciate these quilts!" she said. "She'd probably be backward enough to put them to everyday use."

"I reckon she would," I said. "God knows I been savage 'em for long enough with nobody using 'em. I hope she will! " I didn't want to bring up how I had offered Dee (Wangero) a quilt when she went away to college. Then she had told me they were old-fashioned, out of style.

"But they're priceless!" she was saying now, furiously, for she has a temper. "Maggie would put them on the bed and in five years they'd be in rags. Less than that!" "She can always make some more," I said. "Maggie knows how to quilt. "

Dee (Wangero) looked at me with hatred. "You just will not understand. The point is these quilts, these quilts!"

"Well," I said, stumped. "What would you do with them?"

"Hang them," she said. As it that was the only thing you could do with quilts.

Maggie by now was standing in the door. I could almost hear the sound her feet made as they scraped over each other.

"She can have them, Mama," she said like somebody used to never winning anything, or having anything reserved for her. "I can 'member Grandma Dee without the quilts."

I looked at her hard. She had filled her bottom lip with checkerberry snuff and it gave her face a kind of dopey, hangdog look. It was Grandma Dee and Big Dee who taught her how to quilt herself. She stood there with her scarred hands hidden in the folds of her skirt. She looked at her sister with something like fear but she wasn't mad at her. This was Maggie's portion. This was the way she knew God to work.

When I looked at her like that something hit me in the top of my head and ran down to the soles of my feet. Just like when I'm in church and the spirit of God touches me and I get happy and shout. I did something I never had done before: hugged Maggie to me, then dragged her on into the room, snatched the quilts out of Miss Wangero's hands and dumped them into Maggie's lap. Maggie just sat there on my bed with her mouth open.

"Take one or two of the others," I said to Dee.

But she turned without a word and went out to Hakim-a-barber.

"You just don't understand," she said, as Maggie and I came out to the car.

"What don't I understand?" I wanted to know.

"Your heritage," she said. And then she turned to Maggie, kissed her, and said, "You ought to try to make some-thing of yourself, too, Maggie. It's really a new day for us. But from the way you and Mama still live you'd never know it."

She put on some sunglasses that hid everything above the tip of her nose and her chin.

Maggie smiled; maybe at the sunglasses. But a real mile, not scared. After we watched the car dust settle I asked Maggie to bring me a dip of snuff. And then the two of us sat there just enjoying, until it was time to go in the house and go to bed.

NOTES

1. "made it"：成功

2. Johnny Carson：美国的一名脱口秀节目主持人

3. hooked：被牛角撞伤（为奶牛挤奶的时候）

4. Jimmy T："T"是姓氏的首字母

5. "Wa-su-zo-Tean-o!"：非洲本土问候语的英语谐音

6. "Asalamalakim"：穆斯林问候语的英语谐音

7. Polaroid：宝丽来（一种快速成像的相机）

8. the Civil War：美国内战（1861—1865），又称为南北战争

9. branches：由同一个祖先繁衍而来的家族分支

10. Ream it out again：复述

11. Chitlins：又写作"chitlings"或者"chitterlings"；猪肠（非裔美国人的日常食材）

12. rump prints：人们年长日久的使用留下的臀印

13. sink：由于长时间使用而留下的指痕

Questions for discussion:

1. Why did Wangero (Dee) change her opinions about the African American tradition?

2. Do you agree with Wangero (Dee)'s ideas about traditional cultural heritage?

3. Can you infer Alice Walker's attitude about traditional cultural heritage?

5.5   Appreciation of Selected Readings

爱丽丝·沃克在《祖母的日用家当》（*Everyday Use for Your Grandmama*）中，描述了 20 世纪 60 年代，一个普通的美国黑人家庭母女三人之间的关系和对于黑人传统文化观念的差异。

故事以大女儿（Dee/Wangero）的返家之旅开篇，故事前半部分通过母亲的视角描述了受到白人教育思想影响的大女儿对于美国黑人传统生活方式的厌恶。但是，大女儿此次的返乡的表现与母亲的回忆大相径庭。她对于家中的一切都表现出了极大的兴趣，包括家中的房子、母亲准备的传统食物以及家里的日常使用家

当，她几乎要将厨房里的所有日常家当都收入囊中。

故事的高潮部分围绕两床被子（quilts）展开。被子在美国黑人文化中具有特殊的地位：制作被子的布料是从旧衣服、旧被子上一块块裁剪而成，它体现了黑人女性变废为宝的创意；由于被子需要手工缝制且工作量大，通常由家族中的黑人女性共同完成，体现了黑人女性之间的姐妹情谊；同时，被子还会代代相传，承载了对于家族已故亲人的怀念。故事中的两床被子是母亲为小女儿（Maggie）准备的嫁妆，而 Dee 想把两床被子据为己有。Dee 认为妹妹（Maggie）不懂得欣赏，只会将被子用于日常生活，过几年被子就会变得毫无价值。妈妈却认为，Maggie 已经学会了如何制作被子，她以后会缝制出新的被子。故事的矛盾由此凸显：究竟是将传统文化融入生活还是将传统文化用于文化物品的展示？

美国黑人文化运动颂扬的口号便是"Black is beautiful!"。受到美国黑人文化运动的影响，Dee 表现出了对黑人传统文化物件的极大兴趣。但是 Dee 更注重对黑人传统文化物件的占有和炫耀，没有真正理解传统文化的本质。正如她改名字、改变服饰风格一样，她对于传统文化的认知停留于表面。虽然妈妈和妹妹由于地域限制和教育背景的局限，对外界发生的政治文化运动并不了解，但是她们用自己的生活方式传承了传统文化，将它融入日常生活。

故事中体现出来的两种不同的文化观念都有一定的不足：妈妈和 Maggie 缺乏对传统文化的认知，也没有对于自身文化的自信；Dee 虽然对黑人文化的重要性有认知，却不知如何去传承它。

文化自信是一个国家、一个民族发展中更基本、更深沉、更持久的力量。树立正确的传统文化观对于树立国家和民族的文化自信至关重要。我们不仅要了解中华民族的传统文化的精髓，还要学会如何传承传统文化，要树立理解、保护、传承的多重文化观。

5.6　Supplementary Reading

The Lottery

by Shelley Jackson

The morning of June 27th was clear and sunny, with the fresh warmth of a full-summer day; the flowers were blossoming profusely and the grass was richly green. The people of the village began to gather in the square, between the post office and the bank, around ten o'clock; in some towns there were so many people that the lottery took two days and had to be started on June 26th. but in this village, where there were only about three hundred people, the whole lottery took less than two hours, so it could begin at ten o'clock in the morning and still be through in time to allow the villagers to get home for noon dinner.

　　The children assembled first, of course. School was recently over for the summer, and the feeling of liberty sat uneasily on most of them; they tended to gather together quietly for a while before they broke into boisterous play. and their talk was still of the classroom and the teacher, of books and reprimands. Bobby Martin had already stuffed his pockets full of stones, and the other boys soon followed his example, selecting the smoothest and roundest stones; Bobby and Harry Jones and Dickie Delacroix—the villagers pronounced this name "Dellacroy"—eventually made a great pile of stones in one corner of the square and guarded it against the raids of the other boys. The girls stood aside, talking among themselves, looking over their shoulders at rolled in the dust or clung to the hands of their older brothers or sisters.

　　Soon the men began to gather. surveying their own children, speaking of plantingand rain, tractors and taxes. They stood together, away from the pile of stones in the corner, and their jokes were quiet and they smiled rather than laughed. The women, wearing faded house dresses and sweaters, came shortly after their menfolk. They greeted one another and exchanged bits of gossip as they went to join their husbands. Soon the women, standing by their husbands, began to call to their children, and the children came reluctantly, having to be called four or five times. Bobby Martin ducked under his mother's grasping hand and ran, laughing, back to the pile of stones. His father spoke up sharply, and Bobby came quickly and took his place between his father and his oldest brother.

　　The lottery was conducted—as were the square dances, the teen club, the Halloween program—by Mr. Summers, who had time and energy to devote to civic activities. He was a round-faced, jovial man and he ran the coal business, and people were sorry for him because he had no children and his wife was a scold. When he arrived in the square, carrying the black wooden box, there was a murmur of conversation among the villagers, and he waved and called. "Little late today, folks." The postmaster, Mr. Graves, followed him, carrying a three-legged stool, and the stool was put in the center of the square and Mr. Summers set the black box down on it. The villagers kept their distance, leaving a space between themselves and the stool. and when Mr. Summers said, "Some of you fellows want to give me a hand?" there was a hesitation before two men. Mr. Martin and his oldest son, Baxter. came forward to hold the box steady on the stool while Mr. Summers stirred up the papers inside it.

The original paraphernalia for the lottery had been lost long ago, and the black box now resting on the stool had been put into use even before Old Man Warner, the oldest man in town, was born. Mr. Summers spoke frequently to the villagers about making a new box, but no one liked to upset even as much tradition as was represented by the black box. There was a story that the present box had been made with some pieces of the box that had preceded it, the one that had been constructed when the first people settled down to make a village here. Every year, after the lottery, Mr. Summers began talking again about a new box, but every year the subject was allowed to fade off without anything's being done. The black box grew shabbier each year: by now it was no longer completely black but splintered badly along one side to show the original wood color, and in some places faded or stained.

Mr. Martin and his oldest son, Baxter, held the black box securely on the stool until Mr. Summers had stirred the papers thoroughly with his hand. Because so much of the ritual had been forgotten or discarded, Mr. Summers had been successful in having slips of paper substituted for the chips of wood that had been used for generations. Chips of wood, Mr. Summers had argued. had been all very well when the village was tiny, but now that the population was more than three hundred and likely to keep on growing, it was necessary to use something that would fit more easily into he black box. The night before the lottery, Mr. Summers and Mr. Graves made up the slips of paper and put them in the box, and it was then taken to the safe of Mr. Summers' coal company and locked up until Mr. Summers was ready to take it to the square next morning. The rest of the year, the box was put way, sometimes one place, sometimes another; it had spent one year in Mr. Graves's barn and another year underfoot in the post office. and sometimes it was set on a shelf in the Martin grocery and left there.

There was a great deal of fussing to be done before Mr. Summers declared the lottery open. There were the lists to make up--of heads of families. heads of households in each family. members of each household in each family. There was the proper swearing-in of Mr. Summers by the postmaster, as the official of the lottery; at one time, some people remembered, there had been a recital of some sort, performed by the official of the lottery, a perfunctory. tuneless chant that had been rattled off duly each year; some people believed that the official of the lottery used to stand just so when he said or sang it, others believed that he was supposed to walk among the people, but years and years ago this p3rt of the ritual had been allowed to lapse. There had been, also, a ritual salute, which the official of the lottery had had to use in addressing each person who came up to draw from the box, but this also had changed with time, until now it was felt necessary only for the official to speak to each person approaching. Mr. Summers was very good at all this; in his clean white shirt and blue jeans. with one hand resting carelessly on the black box. he seemed very proper and important as he talked interminably to Mr. Graves and the Martins.

Just as Mr. Summers finally left off talking and turned to the assembled villagers, Mrs. Hutchinson came hurriedly along the path to the square, her sweater thrown over her shoulders, and slid into place in the back of the crowd. "Clean forgot what day it was," she said to Mrs. Delacroix, who stood next to her, and they both laughed softly. "Thought my old man was out back stacking wood," Mrs. Hutchinson went on. "and then I looked out the window and the kids was gone, and then I remembered it was the twenty-seventh and came a-running." She dried her hands on her apron, and Mrs. Delacroix said, "You're in time, though. They're still talking away up there."

Mrs. Hutchinson craned her neck to see through the crowd and found her husband and children standing near the front. She tapped Mrs. Delacroix on the arm as a farewell and began to make her way through the crowd. The people separated good-humoredly to let her through: two or three people said. in voices just loud enough to be heard across the crowd, "Here comes your, Missus, Hutchinson," and "Bill, she made it after all." Mrs. Hutchinson reached her husband, and Mr. Summers, who had been waiting, said cheerfully. "Thought we were going to have to get on without you, Tessie." Mrs. Hutchinson said. grinning, "Wouldn't have me leave m'dishes in the sink, now, would you. Joe?," and soft laughter ran through the crowd as the people stirred back into position after Mrs. Hutchinson's arrival.

"Well, now." Mr. Summers said soberly, "guess we better get started, get this over with, so's we can go back to work. Anybody ain't here?"

"Dunbar." several people said. "Dunbar. Dunbar."

Mr. Summers consulted his list. "Clyde Dunbar." he said. "That's right. He's broke his leg, hasn't he? Who's drawing for him?"

"Me. I guess," a woman said. and Mr. Summers turned to look at her. "Wife draws for her husband." Mr. Summers said. "Don't you have a grown boy to do it for you, Janey?" Although Mr. Summers and everyone else in the village knew the answer perfectly well, it was the business of the official of the lottery to ask such questions formally. Mr. Summers waited with an expression of polite interest while Mrs. Dunbar answered.

"Horace's not but sixteen yet." Mrs. Dunbar said regretfully. "Guess I gotta fill in for the old man this year."

"Right." Sr. Summers said. He made a note on the list he was holding. Then he asked, "Watson boy drawing this year?"

A tall boy in the crowd raised his hand. "Here," he said. "I'm drawing for my mother and me." He blinked his eyes nervously and ducked his head as several voices in the crowd said things like "Good fellow, lack." and "Glad to see your mother's got a man to do it."

"Well," Mr. Summers said, "guess that's everyone. Old Man Warner make it?"

"Here," a voice said, and Mr. Summers nodded.

A sudden hush fell on the crowd as Mr. Summers cleared his throat and looked at the list. "All ready?" he called. "Now, I'll read the names--heads of families first--and the men come up and take a paper out of the box. Keep the paper folded in your hand without looking at it until everyone has had a turn. Everything clear?"

The people had done it so many times that they only half listened to the directions: most of them were quiet. wetting their lips. not looking around. Then Mr. Summers raised one hand high and said, "Adams." A man disengaged himself from the crowd and came forward. "Hi. Steve." Mr. Summers said. and Mr. Adams said. "Hi. Joe." They grinned at one another humorlessly and nervously. Then Mr. Adams reached into the black box and took out a folded paper. He held it firmly by one corner as he turned and went hastily back to his place in the crowd. where he stood a little apart from his family. not looking down at his hand.

"Allen." Mr. Summers said. "Anderson... Bentham."

"Seems like there's no time at all between lotteries any more." Mrs. Delacroix said to Mrs. Graves in the back row.

"Seems like we got through with the last one only last week."

"Time sure goes fast." Mrs. Graves said.

"Clark... Delacroix."

"There goes my old man." Mrs. Delacroix said. She held her breath while her husband went forward.

"Dunbar," Mr. Summers said, and Mrs. Dunbar went steadily to the box while one of the women said. "Go on. Janey," and another said, "There she goes."

"We're next." Mrs. Graves said. She watched while Mr. Graves came around from the side of the box, greeted Mr. Summers gravely and selected a slip of paper from the box. By now, all through the crowd there were men holding the small folded papers in their large hand. turning them over and over nervously Mrs. Dunbar and her two sons stood together, Mrs. Dunbar holding the slip of paper.

"Harburt... Hutchinson."

"Get up there, Bill," Mrs. Hutchinson said. and the people near her laughed.

"Jones."

"They do say," Mr. Adams said to Old Man Warner, who stood next to him, "that over in the north village they're talking of giving up the lottery."

Old Man Warner snorted. "Pack of crazy fools," he said. "Listening to the young folks, nothing's good enough for them. Next thing you know, they'll be wanting to go back to living in caves, nobody works anymore, live that way for a while. Used to be a saying about 'Lottery in June, corn be heavy soon.' First thing you know, we'd all be eating stewed chickweed and acorns. There's always been a lottery," he added petulantly. "Bad enough to see young Joe Summers up there joking with everybody."

"Some places have already quit lotteries." Mrs. Adams said.

"Nothing but trouble in that," Old Man Warner said stoutly. "Pack of young fools."

"Martin." And Bobby Martin watched his father go forward. "Overdyke...Percy."

"I wish they'd hurry," Mrs. Dunbar said to her older son. "I wish they'd hurry."

"They're almost through," her son said.

"You get ready to run tell Dad," Mrs. Dunbar said.

Mr. Summers called his own name and then stepped forward precisely and selected a slip from the box. Then he called,"Warner."

"Seventy-seventh year I been in the lottery," Old Man Warner said as he went through the crowd. "Seventy-seventh time."

"Watson" The tall boy came awkwardly through the crowd. Someone said, "Don't be nervous, Jack," and Mr. Summers said, "Take your time, son."

"Zanini."

After that, there was a long pause, a breathless pause, until Mr. Summers. holding his slip of paper in the air, said, "All right, fellows." For a minute, no one moved, and then all the slips of paper were opened. Suddenly, all the women began to speak at once, saving. "Who is it?," "Who's got it?" "Is it the Dunbars?" "Is it the Watsons?" Then the voices began to say, "It's Hutchinson. It's Bill." "Bill Hutchinson's got it."

"Go tell your father," Mrs. Dunbar said to her older son.

People began to look around to see the Hutchinsons. Bill Hutchinson was standing quiet, staring down at the paper in his hand. Suddenly. Tessie Hutchinson shouted to Mr. Summers. "You didn't give him time enough to take any paper he wanted. I saw you. It wasn't fair!"

"Be a good sport, Tessie." Mrs. Delacroix called, and Mrs. Graves said, "All of us took the same chance." "Shut up, Tessie," Bill Hutchinson said.

"Well, everyone," Mr. Summers said, "that was done pretty fast, and now we've got to be hurrying a little more to get done in time." He consulted his next list. "Bill," he said, "you draw for the Hutchinson family. You got any other households in the Hutchinsons?"

"There's Don and Eva," Mrs. Hutchinson yelled. "Make them take their chance!"

"Daughters draw with their husbands' families, Tessie," Mr. Summers said gently. "You know that as well as anyone else."

"It wasn't fair," Tessie said.

"I guess not, Joe." Bill Hutchinson said regretfully. "My daughter draws with her husband's family; that's only fair. And I've got no other family except the kids."

"Then, as far as drawing for families is concerned, it's you," Mr. Summers said in explanation, "and as far as drawing for households is concerned, that's you, too. Right?"

"Right," Bill Hutchinson said.

"How many kids, Bill?" Mr. Summers asked formally.

"Three," Bill Hutchinson said.

"There's Bill, Jr., and Nancy, and little Dave. And Tessie and me."

"All right, then," Mr. Summers said. "Harry, you got their tickets back?"

Mr. Graves nodded and held up the slips of paper. "Put them in the box, then," Mr. Summers directed. "Take Bill's and put it in."

"I think we ought to start over," Mrs. Hutchinson said, as quietly as she could. "I tell you it wasn't fair. You didn't give him time enough to choose. Everybody saw that."

Mr. Graves had selected the five slips and put them in the box. and he dropped all the papers but those onto the ground. where the breeze caught them and lifted them off.

"Listen, everybody," Mrs. Hutchinson was saying to the people around her.

"Ready, Bill?" Mr. Summers asked. and Bill Hutchinson, with one quick glance around at his wife and children. nodded.

"Remember," Mr. Summers said. "Take the slips and keep them folded until each person has taken one. Harry, you help little Dave." Mr. Graves took the hand of the little boy, who came willingly with him up to the box. "Take a paper out of the box, Davy." Mr. Summers said. Davy put his hand into the box and laughed. "Take just one paper." Mr. Summers said. "Harry, you hold it for him." Mr. Graves took the child's hand and removed the folded paper from the tight fist and held it while little Dave stood next to him and looked up at him wonderingly.

"Nancy next," Mr. Summers said. Nancy was twelve, and her school friends breathed heavily as she went forward switching her skirt, and took a slip daintily from the box "Bill, Jr.," Mr. Summers said, and Billy, his face red and his feet overlarge, near knocked the box over as he got a paper out. "Tessie," Mr. Summers said. She hesitated for a minute, looking around defiantly. and then set her lips and went up to the box. She snatched a paper out and held it behind her.

"Bill," Mr. Summers said, and Bill Hutchinson reached into the box and felt around, bringing his hand out at last with the slip of paper in it.

The crowd was quiet.

A girl whispered A girl whispered "I hope it's not Nancy." "It's not the way it used to be." Old Man Warner said clearly.

"People ain't the way they used to be."

"All right," Mr. Summers said. "Open the papers. Harry, you open little Dave's."

Mr. Graves opened the slip of paper and there was a general sigh through the crowd as he held it up and everyone could see that it was blank. Nancy and Bill Jr. opened theirs at the same time and both beamed and laughed. turning around to the crowd and holding their slips of paper above their heads.

"Tessie," Mr. Summers said. There was a pause, and then Mr. Summers looked at Bill Hutchinson, and Bill unfolded his paper and showed it. It was blank.

"It's Tessie," Mr. Summers said, and his voice was hushed. "Show us her paper Bill." Bill Hutchinson went over to his wife and forced the slip of paper out of her hand. It had a black spot on it, the black spot Mr. Summers had made the night before with the heavy pencil in the coal company office. Bill Hutchinson held it up, and there was a stir in the crowd.

"All right, folks." Mr. Summers said. "Let's finish quickly."

Although the villagers had forgotten the ritual and lost the original black box, they still remembered to use stones. The pile of stones the boys had made earlier was ready; there were stones on the ground with the blowing scraps of paper that had come out of the box Delacroix selected a stone so large she had to pick it up with both hands and turned to Mrs. Dunbar. "Come on," she said. "Hurry up."

Mr. Dunbar had small stones in both hands, and she said, gasping for breath. "I can't run at all. You'll have to go ahead and I'll catch up with you."

The children had stones already. And someone gave little Davy Hutchinson few pebbles.

Tessie Hutchinson was in the center of a cleared space by now, and she held her hands out desperately as the villagers moved in on her. "It isn't fair," she said. A stone hit her on the side of the head. Old Man Warner was saying, "Come on, come on, everyone." Steve Adams was in the front of the crowd of villagers, with Mrs. Graves beside him.

"It isn't fair, it isn't right," Mrs. Hutchinson screamed, and then they were upon her.

Poetry

Unit 1   General Introduction to Poetry

Poetry is as universal as language and almost as ancient. The most primitive peoples in the world have used it, and the most civilized people have cultivated it. Throughout history, people from all walks of life have written poetry, like soldiers, statesmen, lawyers, farmers, scientists, clergy man and so on. It is evident that poetry, as an indispensable part of literature in any country, is gaining an ever-increasing popularity in the intellectual sphere. In literary history, it has been the concern of the most educated, intelligent, and sensitive. In its simpler form, it even appeals to the uneducated and children. Why? Because poetry has given pleasure to people. In the ancient times, poetry was created in oral form and passed down mouth by mouth. People read it, listen to it, and recite it, because poetry provides enjoyment to them. Besides pleasure, some people regard it as something central to their existence, something having unique value to the fully realized life, something that one is better off for having spiritually impoverished without. To understand people's fondness for poetry, we should first define poetry.

However, no one can adequately define it. People have been more successful in appreciating poetry than in defining it. Samuel Taylor Coleridge called poetry, "the best words in the best order." William Wordsworth said, "Poetry is the spontaneous overflow of powerful feelings; it takes its origin from emotion recollected in tranquility." P.B. Shelley stated, "Poetry, in a general sense, maybe defined to be the expression of the imagination." Dylan Thomas called his making of poetry a "Sullen Art". The average readers see poetry as, "the literature that is written in some kind of verse form." Robert Frost made a classic definition, "Poetry is the kind of thing poets write."

Generally speaking, poetry has the following characteristics: a musical effect created by rhythm and sounds, a precise and fresh imagery, and multiple levels of interpretation suggested by the connotation of the loser words and by allusions (Hongxin Jiang, 2004: 2). In this chapter, types of poetry, elements of poetry and rhetorical devices in poetry will be discussed separately.

Unit 2　Types of Poetry: Poetic Writings in Renaissance

2.1　Types of Poetry

There are generally three types of poetry when its meter is considered: rhymed verse, blank verse and free verse. **Rhymed verse** is the most commonly used form of verse and generally has a distinguishable meter and an end rhyme. **Blank verse** is a type of poetry having regular meter (iambic pentameter) but no rhyme. It is one of the most common metrical patterns in English poetry, seen in Shakespeare's dramas and Milton's *Paradise Lost.* **Free verse** is a type of poetry written without the use of strict meter or rhyme, but that is still recognizable as poetry.

As far as the content is concerned, there are three main kinds of poetry: narrative poetry, lyric poetry and dramatic poetry.

Narrative poetry, the oldest type of poetry, is concerned with the telling of a story by giving a verbal representation of a sequence of connected events and propelling characters through a plot. Broadly speaking, it subsumes epic poetry, but is often reserved for smaller works, and with more appeal to human interest. It includes epic, ballad and romance. **Epic** is a major form of narrative literature. It concerns events of a heroic or important nature to the culture of the time and recounts, in a continuous narrative, the life and works of a heroic or mythological person or group of persons. *Beowulf* is one of the longest national epics of the Anglo-Saxon people. **Ballad** is a narrative poem of folk song which tells a story in simple colloquial language, usually in four-line stanzas with the second and fourth lines rhymed. Robinhood Ballads were prevailing in the common people in the Middle Ages of English society. **Romance** is another type of narrative poetry, which involves a primarily medieval fiction in verse or prose dealing with adventures of chivalry and love. It enjoys a French origin in feudal system. *Sir Gawain and the Green Knight* and *Le Morte D' Arthur* are two typical examples.

Lyric Poetry, taking its name from songs sung by individuals or chorus accompanied by the lyre, does not attempt to tell a story but instead is of a more personal nature. They tend to be shorter, melodic, and contemplative. It portrays the poet's own feelings, states of mind, and perceptions rather than characters and actions. It has six major types: sonnet, ode, song, elegy and dirge. **Sonnet** is a fourteen-line poem, written in iambic pentameter (lines with ten syllables, with accents falling on every second syllable). It was introduced to England by Thomas Wyatt, Henry Howard. Spenserian sonnet and Shakespearean sonnet are full of vigor in in English Renaissance period. **Ode** is a form of lyric poem in which the poet highly celebrates a person, a thing or an event. Shelley's *Ode to the West Wind* and Keats' *Ode to Autumn* are the representative odes in English literature. **Song** is a short lyric poem intended to be set to music in either vocal performance or with accompaniment of musical instruments. Ben Jonson's *Song: To Celia* is a typical example. **Elegy** is written in couplets consisting of a hexameter line followed by a pentameter line. It is usually a reflective poem of lamentation or regret, with no set metrical form, generally of melancholy tone, often on death. Thomas Gray's "Elegy Written in a Country Churchyard" is a famous elegy of sentimentalism. And **Dirge** is originally a religious service in honor of the dead. Now it refers to any song of mourning, and is shorter and less formal than an elegy, and often represented as a text meant to be sung aloud. "Full Fathom Five" from *The Tempest* by William Shakespeare is a typical example. Another type of lyrics is called **Pastoral**. It is an artistic composition dealing with the life of shepherds, romanticizing the ideals of the simple rural existence, describing the simplicity, the charm and the serenity of living in the countryside. It places the kindly rural people in the nature-centered activities., like William Wordsworth's *Michael: A Pastoral Poem.*

Dramatic poetry is any verse written for the stage. It applies the discourse of the characters involved to tell a story or portray a situation or to present the voice of an imaginary character speaking directly. One typical example can be seen from the dramatic monologue in Robert Browning's *My Last Duchess.*

There are also other types of poetry, like descriptive poetry, reflective poetry, didactic poetry, and satirical poetry.

Among the most common forms of poetry, popular from the late Middle Ages on, is the **sonnet**, which by the 13th century had become standardized as fourteen lines following a set rhyme scheme and logical structure. By the 14th century and the Italian

Renaissance, the form had further crystallized under the pen of Petrarch, whose sonnets were later translated in the 16th century by Sir Thomas Wyatt, who is credited with introducing the sonnet form into English literature. A traditional Italian or Petrarchan sonnet follows the rhyme scheme of *ABBA, ABBA, CDECDE*. William Wordsworth's *Composed Upon Westminster Bridge*, in which he celebrates the beauty of London, is a famous example of a *Petrarchan/Italian sonnet*. Along with the Petrarchan sonnet, the Shakespearean sonnet, sometimes referred to as "Elizabethan" or "English" sonnet, is one of the best-known and most popular sonnets to this day. It follows the pattern of *ABAB, CDCD, EFEF, GG*, in which the last two lines are a rhyming couplet as you can see from Sonnet 18 by William Shakespeare.

2.2　Edmund Spencer and William Shakespeare

Edmund Spenser (1552—1599) was born in East Smithfield, London. Spenser was called "the Poet's Poet" by Charles Lamb. As a young boy, he was educated in London at the Merchant Taylors' School and matriculated as a sizar at Pembroke College, Cambridge. In 1578, he became for a short time secretary to John Young, Bishop of Rochester. In 1579, he published *The Shepheardes Calender* and around the same time married his first wife, Machabyas Childe. By 1594, Spenser's first wife had died, and in that year he married a much younger Elizabeth Boyle, a relative of Richard Boyle, 1st Earl of Cork. He addressed to her the sonnet sequence *Amoretti. The Shepheardes Calender* is Edmund Spenser's first major work, which appeared in 1579. Spenser's masterpiece is *The Faerie Queene*, an epic poem and fantastical allegory celebrating the Tudor dynasty and Elizabeth I. Spenser originally indicated that he intended the poem to consist of twelve books, the first three books of it were published in 1590, and a second set of three books were published in 1596. In Spenser's "A Letter of the Authors", he states that the entire epic poem is "cloudily enwrapped in allegorical devises", and that the aim behind it was to "fashion a gentleman or noble person in virtuous and gentle discipline".

William Shakespeare (1564—1616) was an English playwright, poet, and actor, and was widely regarded as the greatest writer in the English language and the world's greatest dramatist. He was the third of John and Mary Shakespeare's eight children, and their oldest surviving child. At the age of 18, he married Anne Hathaway, with whom he had three children: Susanna and twins Hamnet and Judith. Sometime between 1585 and 1592, he began a successful career in London as an actor, writer, and part-owner of a playing company called the Lord Chamberlain's Men, later known as the King's Men. At age 49 (around 1613), he appears to have retired to Stratford, where he died three years later. His extant works, including collaborations, consist of some 39 plays, 154 sonnets, two long narrative poems, and a few other verses. In 1609 appeared *Shakespeare's Sonnets. Never before Imprinted.* It is a collections of 154 sonnets. Dedicated to a "Mr. W. H.", these poems were grouped into two contrasting series: one about conflicted love for the "fair youth" and another about uncontrollable lust for the "dark lady", a married woman of dark hair and complexion, Critics have long been praising the *Sonnets* as a profound meditation on the nature of love, sexual passion, procreation, death, and time.

2.3　Introduction to the Selected Poems

As a love sonnet, "***Amoretti LXXV: One Day I Wrote her Name***" highlights the importance of written works that makes people immortal. With its factual description of love and mortality, feelings, desires, and emotions of the two lovers are vividly revealed. It presents two lovers, one of whom desires to make his love mortal. When the speaker has written his beloved's name on sand twice, the waves erased it. Seeing the impossibility to make the mortals immortal, his beloved mocks him and tells him that he is making futile efforts to make anything charming last forever. But the speaker negates this notion and informs her how she will live forever in his verses. He plans to preserve her incredible goodness in his verses. Thus, their love will remain untouched when death overpowers the entire world. The speaker says that less noble things disappear from the face of the earth. However, his love is so noble to him that it deserves to last long. A common theme in Renaissance emerges in the end of the poem: The poet can make his love live through his poetic lines.

"**Sonnet 18**" by William Shakespeare was first published in 1609 in *The Passionate Pilgrim*. It discusses natural beauty and the capacity of poetry in rendering that beauty into everlasting beauty. It also reflects the humanists' adherence to the beautiful art of writing in conquering the death and preserving the harmony of man and nature.

It begins as the speaker praises his anonymous friend without ostentation, intending to present the image of a perfect being. First, he compares his friend with the summer season, keeping all of its attributes intact. Soon, he realizes that everything on the earth suffers a decline, and he wants his friend to live forever. So, he tries to preserve the beauty of his friend in his precious verses. These eternal verses will pass the gentle image of his friend to the coming generations. He is going to achieve this through his verses, believing in this way, that his friend will be saved from the oblivion that accompanies death and become one with time.

Petrarchan sonnets and Shakespearian sonnets are different, in many ways, with a volta being the most salient. Volta, an Itallian equivalent of a turn in thought in a sonnet, helps the readers to notice a shift in its tone, and more importantly, thoughts by applying such inntial words like But, Yet, or And yet. The readers would find an idea turned on its head, a question answered, or the subject matter further complicated. In the Petrarchan sonnet, the turn tends to fall around the division between the octet and the sestet, while English sonnets usually place it at or near the beginning of the closing couplet.

2.4   Selected Readings

Selected Reading A

Sonnet 75

by Edmund Spenser

One day I wrote her name upon the strand,

But came the waves and wash'ed it away:

Agayne I wrote it with a second hand,

But came the tyde, and made my paynes his pray.

"Vayne man," sayd she, "that doest in vaine assay,

A mortall thing so to immortalize,

For I my selve shall lyke to this decay,

And eek my name bee wyped out lykewize."

"Not so," quod I, "let baser things devize,

To dy in dust, but you shall live by fame:

My verse your vertues rare shall eternize,

And in the heavens wryte your glorious name,

Where whenas death shall all the world wubdew,

Our love shall live, and later life renew."

Selected Reading B

Sonnet 18

by William Shakespeare

Shall I compare thee to a summer's day?

Thou art more lovely and more temperate.

Rough winds do shake the darling buds of May,

And summer's lease hath all too short a date.

Sometime too hot the eye of heaven shines,

And often is his gold complexion dimmed;

And every fair from fair sometime declines,

By chance, or nature's changing course, untrimmed;

But thy eternal summer shall not fade,

Nor lose possession of that fair thou ow'st,

Nor shall death brag thou wand'rest in his shade,

When in eternal lines to Time thou grow'st.

So long as men can breathe, or eyes can see,

So long lives this, and this gives life to thee.

Questions for discussion:

1. Grasp the values of humanism in the Renaissance by understanding the meaning of the sea image and the symbolic meaning of "thee" in poetry.

2. Does Shakespeare have something in common with Chinese literature when he writes "thee" as the idealized embodiment of all good things?

3. Hu Jialuan, a famous Chinese scholar, believes that through the comparison between heaven and man, the poem "fully displays the two popular themes in the Renaissance, the greatness of man and the immortality of literature". What do you think of this view?

2.5　Appreciation of Selected Readings

文艺复兴作为一场席卷了欧洲的思想解放运动，始于意大利，其核心是人文主义，强调人的重要性，提倡人性，反对神性。十四行诗在意大利文艺复兴时期呈现出繁荣兴盛的景象。英国作为工业革命的首发地，创造了巨大生产力，随着国家的君主专制统治的加强，社会秩序变得更加稳定，人们对新的文化产生了强烈的需求。意大利文艺复兴的新思想和创作手法逐渐由翻译家、诗人传到了英国。16 世纪初，十四行诗到英国后，结构发生了变化，变得更适应英语语言特点，因而风行一时。到 16 世纪末，十四行诗已成了英国最流行的诗歌体裁，产生了像锡德尼、斯宾塞这样著名的十四行诗人。莎士比亚进一步丰富和发展了这一诗体，一生写下 154 首十四行诗。他的十四行诗体（又称伊丽莎白体），由 3 个四行的小节（quatrain）加 1 个偶句（couplet）构成，每行 5 个抑扬格音步（iambic pentameter），即一轻一重 10 个音节，韵脚排列为 abab，cdcd，efef，gg。莎士比亚诗歌形象生动、结构巧妙、音乐性强、起承转合自如，常常在最后对偶句中概括全诗内容，点明主题，表达新兴资产阶级理想与情怀。以上两首诗歌中展现了文艺复兴时期的一个重大主题，即诗歌具有战胜时空、使人不朽的强大力量，第一首以恋人之间的对话展开，展示了诗中叙述者面对猛兽般的潮水和恋人无情的嘲讽时，依然相信人因名声和美德而不朽，人因有爱而生命常青的强大力量。第二首通过思辨的方式反映了爱的稳定，美的永恒和诗歌的不朽，一直以来被人们认为是流传最为广泛的一首诗歌。

2.6　Supplementary Reading

Composed upon Westminster Bridge

by　William　Wordsworth

Earth has not anything to show more fair:

Dull would he be of soul who could pass by

A sight so touching in its majesty:

This City now doth, like a garment, wear

The beauty of the morning: silent, bare,

Ships, towers, domes, theatres, and temples lie

Open unto the fields, and to the sky;

All bright and glittering in the smokeless air.

Never did sun more beautifully steep

In his first splendour, valley, rock, or hill;
Ne'er saw I, never felt, a calm so deep!
The river glideth at his own sweet will:
Dear God! the very houses seem asleep;
And all that mighty heart is lying still!

Unit 3　Elements in Poetry: Poetic Writings of Romanticism

Poetry uses forms and conventions to suggest differential interpretations of words, or to evoke emotive responses. Devices such as assonance, alliteration, onomatopoeia, and rhythm may convey musical or incantatory effects. Rhyme, alliteration, assonance and consonance are ways of creating repetitive patterns of sound. They may be used as an independent structural element in a poem, to reinforce rhythmic patterns, or as an ornamental element. They can also carry a meaning separate from the repetitive sound patterns created. For example, Chaucer used heavy alliteration to mock Old English verse and to paint a character as archaic.

3.1　Elements in poetry

Prosody is the study of the meter, rhythm, and intonation of a poem. Rhythm and meter are different, although closely related. Meter is the definitive pattern established for a verse, while rhythm is the actual sound that results from a line of poetry. Prosody also may be used more specifically to refer to the scanning of poetic lines to show meter.

Rhyme consists of identical (hard-rhyme) or similar (soft-rhyme) syllables placed at the ends of lines or at predictable locations within lines (internal rhyme). In terms of the stress pattern it takes, rhyme may assume two types: masculine rhyme and feminine rhyme. With regard to its position in verse lines, rhyme may be classified into end rhyme, initial rhyme and internal rhyme. And in terms of similarity, rhyme may be categorized into perfect and imperfect ones. Languages vary in the richness of their rhyming structures; Italian, for example, has a rich rhyming structure permitting maintenance of a limited set of rhymes throughout a lengthy poem. The richness results from word endings that follow regular forms. English, with its irregular word endings adopted from other languages, is less rich in rhyme. The degree of richness of a language's rhyming structures plays a substantial role in determining what poetic forms are commonly used in that language. **A rhyme scheme** is the pattern of rhyme between lines of a poem or song. It is usually referred to by using letters to indicate which lines rhyme. In other words, it is the pattern of end rhymes or lines. A rhyme scheme gives the scheme of the rhyme; a regular pattern of rhyming words in a poem (the end words). For example, "A, B, A, B," indicates a four-line stanza in which the first and third lines rhyme, as do the second and fourth.

Here is an example of this rhyme scheme from "To Anthea, Who May Command Him Any Thing by Robert Herrick":

Bid me to weep, and I will weep	A
While I have eyes to see;	B
And having none, and yet I will keep	A
A heart to weep for thee.	B

Here are some typical rhyme schemes:

Couplet: "A, A", but usually occurs as "A, A, B, B, C, C, D, D ...".

Petrarchan sonnet: "ABBA ABBA CDE CDE" or "ABBA ABBA CDC DCD".

Shakespearean sonnet: "ABAB CDCD EFEF GG".

Spenserian sonnet: "ABAB BCBC CDCD EE".

Ottava rima: "A,B,A,B,A,B,C,C".

Alliteration, assonance and consonance are ways of creating repetitive patterns of sound. **Alliteration** is the repetition of letters or letter-sounds at the beginning of two or more words immediately succeeding each other, or at short intervals; or the recurrence of the same letter in accented parts of words. Alliteration and assonance played a key role in structuring early Germanic, Norse and Old English forms of poetry. The alliterative patterns of early Germanic poetry interweave meter and alliteration as a key part of their structure, so that the metrical pattern determines when the listener expects instances of alliteration to occur. This can be compared to an ornamental use of alliteration in most Modern European poetry, where alliterative patterns are not formal or carried through full stanzas. Alliteration is particularly useful in languages with less rich rhyming structures. **Assonance**, where the use of similar vowel sounds within a word rather than similar sounds at the beginning or end of a word, was widely used in skaldic poetry but goes back to the Homeric epic. Because verbs carry much of the pitch in the English language, assonance can loosely evoke the tonal elements of Chinese poetry and so is useful in translating Chinese poetry. **Consonance** occurs where a consonant sound is repeated throughout a sentence without putting the sound only at the front of a word. Consonance provokes a more subtle effect than alliteration and so is less useful as a structural element.

Examples: great/**gr**ow, **s**end/**s**it (alliteration); gr**eat**/f**ail**, s**e**nd/b**e**ll (assonance); gr**eat**/m**eat**, se**nd**/ha**nd** (consonance).

Metrical rhythm generally involves precise arrangements of syllables into repeated patterns called feet within a line. In Modern English verse the pattern of stresses primarily differentiates feet, so the most obvious kind of rhythm based on meter in English poetry is often founded on the regular repetition of stressed and unstressed syllables. The rhythm involves meter and foot. **Foot** is the basic unit or pattern of meter in a poetic line. When scanning a line of verse, a poet looks at feet as the basic rhythmic unit rather than words. A foot consists of two or three syllables, one or two of which are stressed. A foot can consist of multiple words and a single word can contain many feet; furthermore, a foot can, and often does, bridge multiple words, containing, for example, the last two syllables of one word and the first of the next. So there are many types of foot:

—Note: "/" for a strong /stressed syllable, "-" for a weak/unstressed syllable

Iambus (-/) e.g. defeat, return (one unstressed syllable + one stressed syllable)

trochee (/-) e.g. listen, double (one stressed syllable + one unstressed syllable)

anapest (--/) e.g. with a leap (two stressed syllable + one unstressed syllable)

dactyl (/--) e.g. merrily, here we go (one stressed syllable + two unstressed syllable)

pyrrhic (--) e.g. the season of mists (two short or unstressed syllables together)

spondee (//) e.g. football (two long or stressed syllables together)

Meters are customarily grouped according to a characteristic metrical foot and the number of feet per line. The number of metrical feet in a line is described in Greek terminology as follows: monometer (one foot), dimeter (two feet), trimeter (three feet), tetrameter (four feet), pentameter (five feet), hexameter (six feet), heptameter (seven feet) and octameter (eight feet).

A verse line is fully measured only when the number and type of feet are named. For example, "iambic pentameter" refers to a meter comprising five feet per line, in which the predominant kind of foot is the "iamb".

"The trum/pet of /a pro/phecy! /O, Wind,

If Win/ter comes, /can Spring /be far /behind?"

In this poem there are five feet in each line, we call it a Pentameter. Similarly, "dactylic hexameter", comprises six feet per line, of which the dominant kind of foot is the "dactyl".

The most common metrical feet in English are: Iambic pentameter, "The curfew tolls the knell of parting day", lines from Thomas Gray's "Elegy Written in a Country Churchyard"; Anapestic tetrameter, "With a leap and a bound the swift Anapests throngs" lines from George Gordon Byron's poem "The Destruction of Sennacherib"; Trochaic pentameter, "There they are, my fifty men and women." lines from Robert Browning's "One Word More"; Dactylic dimeter, "Eve, with her basket, was \ Deep in the bells and grass."lines quoted from Ralph Hodgson's "Eve".

An image is anything that involves one or more of one's five senses, namely, sight, bearing, smell, touch, and taste. In the 20th century Ezra Pound defined an image as an intellectual and emotional complex in an instant time. Typically, images can be classified into two types: literal and figurative. The former type employs concrete, specific and sensory words to appeal to one's sense of realistic perception so as to create a picture. Figurative images do not follow the literal meaning of the words exactly and it contains an extension of the meaning of the words in the use of figures of speech that calls for imagination to create a vague portrait. The word image often suggests a mental picture, something that can be seen in one's inner eyes.

Imagery is used to refer to a pattern of related details in a poem which conveys an idea or feeling beyond what the images literally describe. It usually is the verbal creation or re-creation of an experience in the mind. Imagery can be remembered or imaginary. In other words, it is either something an individual experienced or a corresponding equivalent in the real world. As is strong in conveying vivid, concrete mental impression, imagery is very important in poetry.

3.2　William Wordsworth and Walt Whitman

William Wordsworth (1770—1850) was an English Romantic poet who, with Samuel Taylor Coleridge, helped to launch the Romantic Age in English literature with their joint publication *Lyrical Ballads* in 1798. The second of five children born to John Wordsworth and Ann Cookson, William Wordsworth was born on 7 April 1770. Wordsworth was taught to read by his mother and attended, first, a tiny school of low quality in Cockermouth, then a school in Penrith for the children of upper-class families, instilling in students' traditions that included pursuing both scholarly and local activities. It was at the school in Penrith that he met the Hutchinsons, including Mary, who later became his wife. Wordsworth made his debut as a writer in 1787 when he published a sonnet. That same year he began attending St John's College, Cambridge. He received his BA degree in 1791. The year 1793 saw the first publication of poems by Wordsworth, in the collections *An Evening Walk and Descriptive Sketches*. It was in 1795 that he met Samuel Taylor Coleridge in Somerset. The two poets quickly developed a close friendship. Together Wordsworth and Coleridge (with insights from Dorothy) produced *Lyrical Ballads* (1798), an important work in the English Romantic movement. One of Wordsworth's most famous poems, *Tintern Abbey*, was published in this collection. *The Prelude*, commenced during the harsh winter of 1798, and periodically expanded and revised throughout Wordsworth's life, is generally considered to be Wordsworth's masterpiece and it is autobiographical in essence. For living with Dorothy in Goslar, and latter settling at Dove Cottage in Grasmere in the Lake District. Wordsworth, together with Coleridge and Southey came to be known as the "Lake Poets". Throughout this period many of Wordsworth's poems revolved around themes of death, endurance, separation and grief. His deep love for nature runs through such short lyrics as *Lines Composed A Few Miles above Tintern Abbey* (1798); *She Dwelt among the Untrodden Ways* (1800); *I Wandered Lonely as a Cloud* (also known as Daffodils) (1807); *My Heart Leaps Up* (1807) and *Composed upon Westminster Bridge, September 3, 1802*. Wordsworth succeeded Southey ans English Poet Laureate in 1843.

Walt Whitman was an American poet, essayist, and journalist. He has been claimed as the first "poet of democracy" in the United States and the father of free verse. Whitman was born in Huntington on Long Island on May 31, 1819. As a child and through much of his career he resided in Brooklyn. At age 11, Whitman left formal schooling to go to work. Later, Whitman worked as a journalist, a teacher, and a government clerk. Whitman's major poetry collection, *Leaves of Grass*, was first published in 1855, which was an attempt at reaching out to the common person with an American epic. He continued expanding and revising it until his death in 1892. Whitman intended to write a distinctly American epic and used free verse with a cadence based on the *Bible*. The first volume of poetry was preceded by a prose preface of 827 lines. The succeeding untitled twelve poems totaled 2315 lines—1336 lines belonging to the first untitled poem, later called "Song of Myself". Whitman produced further editions of *Leaves of Grass* in 1876, 1881, and 1889. As the end of 1891 approached, he prepared a final edition of *Leaves of Grass*, a version that has been nicknamed the "Deathbed Edition". Whitman died on March 26, 1892. Two of his well-known poems are "O Captain! My Captain!" and "When Lilacs Last in the Dooryard Bloom'd", which were written on the death of Abraham Lincoln.

3.3 Introduction to the Selected Poems

"I Wandered Lonely as a Cloud", also known as "Daffodils", was first published in 1807. It captures the bewitching beauty of the wildflowers and expresses a deeper feeling and emotions of the poet. It is an eternal classic for describing nature and its scenic beauty.

The poem tells the poet's encounters in detail with the majestic daffodils in the field beside the lake. It ends with ever-mounting impact of nature on a human. Which is triggered by nature, often serves as a delight for the poet, when feeling low or in loneliness.

The poem starts with the description of a lonely cloud, floating in the air over the valleys and hills. Then the poet comes across a group of daffodil flowers beside a lake. Having grown under trees, the flowers were dancing in the morning breeze. This beautiful scene made the poet forget the loneliness brought about by the sight of cloud and see the flowers in their purely natural state. The poet compares the daffodils with stars and states that they continue to shine as if stars in a milky way, reaching the margin of the bay. Now they are thousands that he can see, a host of golden flowers, dancing in the morning breeze like dancers tossing their heads in a trance.

The purely natural scene has been captured in words. The waves have also started dancing along with the flowers. The poet sees that the flowers have sparkled more and have won the competition against the sparkling waves. The poet reveals his happiness in such happy company. He thinks that this wealth of happiness would have never come to him through any other means for natural beauty can bring everlasting happiness.

When the poet is back at home and states that when he is alone and lies down on his couch, he finds himself in a pensive or depressive mood or vacant thoughts. Then his imagination brings the scene of those flowers to his solitude. This blissfulness of solitude fills his heart with pleasure. He feels that he is dancing with the flowers in his imagination and dreams. Thus, the natural scene has brought him to be happy at all times, even in his solitude. This wisdom has come to him with the understanding of nature. So, for the poet, the presence of nature means the arrival of wisdom.

Song of Myself is the "founding" poem of *Leaves of Grass*, appearing as the lead poem in the series of twelve untitled poems of the work's first edition first published in 1855. It is a long narrative poem about the poet's self-discovery. The poem speaks about the narrator's journey, demonstrating the enlightenment of his soul, and pleasure in simple things. It also illustrates nature's crucial role in man's life. The speaker in this poem celebrates himself and all parts of him along with every audience. He begins his journey at the age of thirty-two when he is in perfect health. He invites his soul in his journey and urges nature to negotiate with its original form. To him, "askers" "talkers" and "trippers" are wasting their precious time while discussing societies and discoveries. He advises them to listen to their souls as he listens and enjoys a blissful revelation of his inner self which gives him peace and satisfaction. He narrates his significant meeting with an innocent child who questions him about the grass. His question throws him into the valley of wisdom, where he connects this simple object with divinity.

He also expresses his love for the people of all ages, different sexes, ethnicity, natural objects, and animals. He declares himself the poet of all men and women as he knows that goodness, evil and pain play a significant role in man's life. He even catalogs the sounds he hears and notices the infinite wonders even in the slightest things around him. Toward the end, he makes death as his subject and states that he is not afraid of death because it does not come to put an end to our lives. Rather, it transports us to another place where we get up taking various forms. What, however, enchants the readers is the way he discovers his identity through this mystical journey.

While the concept is about self-discovery, it implies to both individual and universal subjects. The poet notices bravery and heroism in common people instead of legendary heroical characters. The poem has also been an inspiration for other famous literary works.

3.4   Selected Readings

I Wandered Lonely as a Cloud

by William Wordsworth

I wandered lonely as a Cloud
That floats on high o'er Vales and Hills,
When all at once I saw a crowd,
A host, of golden Daffodils;
Beside the lake, beneath the trees,
Fluttering and dancing in the breeze.

Continuous as the stars that shine
And twinkle on the Milky Way,
They stretch'd in never-ending line
Along the margin of a bay:
Ten thousand saw I at a glance,
Tossing their heads in sprightly dance.

The waves beside them danced; but they
Out-did the sparkling waves in glee:—
A poet could not but be gay
In such a jocund company:
I gazed—and gazed—but little thought
What wealth the show to me had brought:

For oft when on my couch I lie

In vacant or in pensive mood,

They flash upon that inward eye

Which is the bliss of solitude,

And then my heart with pleasure fills,

And dances with the Daffodils.

Song of Myself, 51

by Walt Whitman

The past and present wilt—I have fill'd them, emptied them.

And proceed to fill my next fold of the future.

Listener up there! what have you to confide to me?

Look in my face while I snuff the sidle of evening,

(Talk honestly, no one else hears you, and I stay only a minute longer.)

Do I contradict myself?

Very well then I contradict myself,

(I am large, I contain multitudes.)

I concentrate toward them that are nigh, I wait on the door-slab.

Who has done his day's work? who will soonest be through with his supper?

Who wishes to walk with me?

Will you speak before I am gone? will you prove already too late?

Questions for discussion:

1. Look at the two poems and consider whether there is alliteration, rhyme, vowel and consonant in the poem. Please divide the rhythm of poetry.

2. How do you explain "I an large, I contain multitudes."?

3. Walt Whitman brought all American experiences into his poetry and entitled it as *Leaves of Grass* with the purpose to identify his self with the social, or

more specifically with the democratic "En-Masse" of America. Translate the most frequently quoted phrases in China, "青山绿水就是金山银山"和"江山就是人民，人民就是江山" and discuss the profound meaning and enlightenment of these two sentences above in combination with the two poems learned.

3.5   Appreciation of Selected Readings

英国诗人威廉·华兹华斯的《我是一朵孤独的流云》（*I Wandered Lonely as a Cloud*）以"我好似一朵孤独的流云，高高地飘荡在山谷之上"起兴，通过明喻将"我"比作一朵孤云，将诗人内心的孤独寄予"云朵"，唤起人们对人的生存境遇的思考。诗中的云是孤独的，漫无目的的，也是居无定所的。诗人目睹了法国大革命的失败，受到很大的打击，其孤独是心理的、社会的，也是对人的哲思的产物。为了寄意，诗人把"云"作为载体，让孤独意象化，变成一种外在的、可感的形式。孤独或是源自离群索居或是漂泊异乡。由云引发感叹，造就的优秀诗句在中国数不胜数。陶渊明卸下官职后，写下"万族各有托，孤云独无依"的感叹，王维以"行到水穷处，坐看云起时"表达超然物外，回归自然的理想，而李白的"众鸟高飞尽，孤云独去闲"更将逍遥处世之道写到了极致。可以说，孤独的书写具有普遍意义，孤独往往深埋在人的内心深处。该诗又名《水仙》，水仙是一种特别美丽的花，诗人极力歌颂了它的动态美和静态美，展示了孤独中的欢乐。诗中的花让读者尽享优美的湖景，又感悟到自然的和谐之美，诗人借此机会表达了人性的回归，自然和人类和谐相处，这才是一种极乐世界。诗人也正是在这般和谐的自然之家中重新捡起对生活的信心，进而，华兹华斯诗歌中的孤独变成了一种独处中的快乐。大自然深深地影响了诗人，给予诗人的是一个可以疗伤、养心，尽情放纵和狂喜的空间。云寄托的孤独在自然的独处中获得自由，不被世俗的诱惑烦扰，内心获得宁静。《我是一朵孤独的流云》是华兹华斯浪漫主义抒情诗歌的代表之作，全诗以写景和抒情为主。诗人采取三音步抑扬格的形式，韵律为 ABABCC。

惠特曼的《自我之歌》（*Song of Myself*）是一首篇幅较长的自由诗歌，共 52 段，1300 余行。此处选取的是第 51 段。诗人在这首诗歌里的"自我"含义深邃，首先这是讲述诗人自己。诗人在诗歌中以种种自白的倾向，将个人的情况和经历注入诗歌素材中。其次，诗人用"自我"替代了诗中任何一个一般性的叙述者，将普通人置于诗歌的现场来表达自己的感受，展示自己的行动。另外，这个"自我"具有哲学的高度，可理解为万物，或者宇宙自身。此处所选诗歌的第 51 段中，这个"自我"似乎在向"我"的过去和现在告别，去充实未来。诗歌中的这个"我"承认自己是自相矛盾的，因为"我"博大宽广，"我"包罗万象。在这样一个超然的"我"中，诗人似乎又是一个普通的"自我"，因为诗人关注远处的那个聆听者，关注普通人的日常，工作、晚饭、散步，甚至是人们的内心所思所想。作为《草叶集》的开篇之作，该诗集中体出现了诗人的民主思想，正如诗集名称所示，草叶象征了一切平凡之人事。通过阅读该诗，读者们可以看到诗人对普通劳动阶级人民的关注。另外，其诗歌内容豪放粗狂，形式不拘泥于传统，无韵、无节奏，语言取自生活口语，不屑于精工细琢。主题与形式达到了完全不同于传统创作的统一，从而为美国现代主义诗歌开创了新的诗风，其影响超越了诗人所处的时代，也跨越了国界，对我国五四运动后的新诗创作产生了很大的影响。

3.6　Supplementary Reading

If You Were Coming in the Fall

by Emily Dickinson

If you were coming in the fall,
I'd brush the summer by
With half a smile and half a spurn,
As housewives do a fly.

If I could see you in a year,
I'd wind the months in balls,
And put them each in separate drawers,
Until their time befalls.

If only centuries delayed,
I'd count them on my hand,
Subtracting till my fingers dropped
Into Van Diemens land.

If certain, when this life was out,

That yours and mine should be,

I'd toss it yonder like a rind,

And taste eternity.

But now, all ignorant of the length

Of time's uncertain wing,

It goads me, like the goblin bee,

That will not state its sting.

Unit 4 Poetic Devices in Poetry: Poetic Writings of Modernism

Poetry contains "the best words in the best order". In reading poems, it is necessary to know more than what the word or words mean, for the poets often use words figuratively. Figures of speech are often employed in literature to convey special meanings. The use of personification, symbolism, paradox, irony, and other literary devices often leaves a poem open to multiple interpretations. Similarly, figures of speech such as metaphor, simile, and metonymy establish a resonance between otherwise disparate images—a layering of meanings, forming connections previously not perceived. Thus, the "best words" for poets are usually those that imply or suggest; those aim at emphasis, profoundness, vividness, clarity, or freshness of expression. The readers should develop the habit of considering the connotations of words as well as their denotations.

4.1 Poetic Devices in Poetry

Simile is a figure of speech in which two essentially dissimilar objects or concepts are expressly compared with one another through the use of "like" or "as". It is meant to assert similarity with the help of like or as. A proper simile creates an explicit comparison between two things that are different enough from each other such that their comparability appears unlikely. The statement "this poem is like a punch in the gut" features a simile. Figuratively, the simile's comparison and association between these two things establishes that the impact of the poem on the speaker has the force of and feels similar to a punch in the gut. Simile is found in many famous examples of poetry, prose, drama, lyrics. In E.B. white's words, "Like writing with a pen, you can cross out your past but you can't erase it." Life seems to be compared to a pen with the power to deny the pass but incapable of passing the past; and in Robert Burns' poem *A Red, Red Rose*, love refreshes the lover with warm colors and sweet sounds:

Omy Luve's like a red, red rose,

That's newly sprung in June;

O my Luve's like the melodie

That's sweetly play'd in tune.

Simile can create an association between two dissimilar entities or ideas that illuminate each other and enhance the meaning of both. In this stanza, the poet compares the person he loves both to a rose and melody. By comparing his "Luve", an actual person rather than an abstract concept, to a rose and a song, the poet establishes a similarity between two seemingly different things and allows the reader to understand that the poet views the person he loves as a symbol of love itself.

Metaphor, like simile, is another widely known figure of speech on which poetry is founded. Aristotle wrote in the *Poetics* that "the greatest thing by far is to be a master of metaphor." A metaphor makes a comparison between two non-similar things to create implicit comparisons without the express use of "like" or "as". Metaphor is a means of asserting that two things are identical in comparison rather than just similar. It is very useful in literature for using specific images or concepts to state abstract truths. One of the most famous metaphors in literature is featured in this line from William Shakespeare's *Romeo and Juliet*:

"What light through yonder window breaks? It is the East, and Juliet, the sun!"

In this metaphor, Juliet is compared to the sun, Juliet is the sun. The comparison demonstrates the truth that Juliet and the sun are the same in the lover's eyes. They are equally beautiful, awesome, and full of life-giving force and warmth. It seems that metaphors allow writers to create imagery for readers that is limited by description alone. An effective metaphor eliminates the need for excessive explanation or description on the part of the writer.

Conceit is differentiated from simile and metaphor in the degree to which its comparison between things is so unlikely that there must be an imagined connection. Writers often utilize conceit in poetry to link two very different objects, concepts, or ideas. The connection is often surprising and challenging to the reader in its novelty, so it can make a literary work memorable in its appeal to both the intellect and imagination. John Donne, as a metaphysical poet, stands out as the best exponent of the use of metaphysical conceits. In "A Valediction: Forbidding Mourning", he compares his and his beloved's souls with the two legs of a drafting compass, and her soul to the fixed foot, his the other foot, which reminds us of the spiritual union of the two lovers. Because conceits make unusual and unlikely comparisons between two things, they allow readers to look at things in a new way. However, more often than not, it surprises and shocks readers by making farfetched comparisons.

Personification is giving human traits including human attributes and/or feelings to inanimate objects or speaking of it as if it were human. Personification relies on imagination for understanding. It is an interesting, creative, and effective way for a writer to illustrate a concept or make a point. In Edgar Allan Poe's poem "The Raven," the poet skillfully personifies the raven, which only speaks the same word, "nevermore," in response to the narrator's questions. It is vivid and memorable.

Symbolism is another literary device that refers to the use of symbols in a literary work. A symbol usually stands for or suggests something else; it represents something beyond literal meaning. In poems, it can be a word, object, action, character, or concept that embodies and evokes a range of additional meaning and significance. In the poem "Fire and Ice", Robert Frost utilizes symbolism to indicate to readers how the world may be destroyed:

Some say the world will end in fire,

Some say in ice.

From what I've tasted of desire

I hold with those who favor fire.

But if it had to perish twice,

I think I know enough of hate.

To say that for destruction ice,

Is also great.

And would suffice.

In this poem, while "fire" symbolizes destructive and consuming emotions such as jealousy, desire for power, anger, and impulsivity, "ice" symbolizes destructive and withholding emotions such as hate, indifference, loneliness, and isolation. It's the symbolism of fire and ice that enhances the meaning and significance of the poem.

Paradox is a statement that appears at first to be contradictory, but upon reflection then makes sense. This literary device is commonly used to engage a reader to discover an underlying logic in a seemingly self-contradictory statement. As a result, it calls for readers to understand concepts in a different and even non-traditional way, like "The Pen is Mightier than the Sword". As a literary device, it sets up a situation, idea, or concept that appears on the surface to be contradictory or impossible, and opens up to a discovery of an underlying truth.

Oxymoron differs from paradox in pairing two words together that are opposing and/or contradictory, so it gains the name, being a "condensed" paradox. Oxymoron has the effect of creating an impression, enhancing a concept, and even entertaining the reader. These word pairings are not inherently opposite, but their individual concepts can seem contradictory when combined. A classic example comes from the play, *Romeo and Juliet*:

"Good night, good night! parting is such sweet sorrow,

That I shall say good night till it be morrow."

In perhaps the most well-known oxymoron in literature, Juliet describes her feelings about Romeo leaving her presence as "sweet sorrow." It indicates that Juliet's "sorrow" and sadness at the thought that Romeo must part from her is also "sweet" and pleasant. She feels sadness knowing she must say good night to Romeo. However, she lovingly anticipates seeing him again which is a pleasant feeling.

Irony is a literary device which involves a contradiction between appearance and reality. An ironic statement is different from what appears to be true. Many common phrases and situations reflect irony.

Allusion is also a type of poetic device. To allude is to refer to something without explaining it, to hint at it. So, allusion is not explained, it depends on the reader knowing whatever external thing to which the author is alluding. T. S. Eliot's poem, "The Waste Land", is widely considered by scholars and academics to be one of the most important poems of the 20th century. It is so densely packed with allusions that most casual readers find it to be impenetrable.

4.2   T.S. Eliot

Thomas Stearns Eliot (1888—1965) was an American- English poet, playwright, literary critic, editor and a leader of the modernist movement in poetry. He was born in St. Louis, Missouri, of an old New England family. He was educated at Harvard before moving to England in 1914, where he would work as an editor from the early 1920s until his death. His first important poem, and the first modernist masterpiece in English, was the radically experimental *The Love Song of J. Alfred Prufrock* (1917). *The Waste Land* (1922) made his international reputation by expressing with startling power the disillusionment of the postwar years. Eliot's other poetic works include *Four Quartets* (1943) and *Ash Wednesday* (1930). His plays, *Murder in the Cathedral* (1935), *The Family Reunion* (1939), *The Cocktail Party* (1949), *The Confidential Clerk* (1954), and *The Elder Statesman* (1959) were published in one volume in 1962; Collected Poems 1909-62 appeared in 1963. In the essay *Tradition and the Individual Talent*, Eliot, as a critic, asserts that tradition is not a mere repetition of the work of the immediate past and the poet writing in English may also make his own tradition by using materials from any past period, in any language.

Eliot's poetry is difficult to read, for one thing the images and symbols seem very much disconnected, for another, an obvious source of difficulty lies in his learned quotations and allusions. Eliot piles up a heap of images, visual, auditory, olfactory, and more for the readers to figure out what is being said. Dramatic monologue used.

4.3   Introduction to *The Love Song of J. Alfred Prufrock*

The Love Song of J. Alfred Prufrock is a lyrical, dramatic monologue of a middle-class male persona who inhabits a physically and spiritually bleak environment. It was first written between 1910—1911 and published in June 1915 and again in 1917.

As a typical dramatic monologue, the poet dramatize the whole situation in this poem by making Prufrock speaks directly to us about his thoughts in leaps and bounds, jumping from one image to another, just as human mind does. As we listen to his monologue and make connections that are not spelled out, we come to understand

Prufrock's paralysis and mental fragmentation hidden from acquaintances, which are symbolic of the modern life.

The poem reflects the thoughts of "J. Alfred Prufrock" searching for love in an uncertain world. Approximately 130 lines long, this poem follows the ramblings of Prufrock, the would-be suitor of an unnamed and nebulously developed woman. Despite knowing what to say and how to express his love, he is hesitant. In his mind, he goes further in his relationship and observation. However, physically he remains in the same place as he continues to talk to another person through his monologue. The poem has gained immense popularity since its publication due to its pseudo-romantic tone.

Irony is the major poetical device in throughout the poem. The title "love song" of the poem sings of no love, but inability to love because of solipsism. The epigraph to "Prufrock" also serves to cast ironic light on Prufrock's intent. Like Guido, Prufrock had intended his story never be told, and so by quoting Guido, Eliot reveals his view of Prufrock's love song. Prufrock himself is suffering from multiple personalities of sorts, and he embodies both Guido and Dante in the Inferno analogy. One is the storyteller; the other the listener who later reveals the story to the world. The role of Dante is filled by you, the reader, as in "Let us go then, you and I". In that, the reader is granted the power to do as he pleases with Prufrock's love song.

The speaker has clear insights into his sterile life but he is lacking in will to change that life. His strong desire for love and his hundred times of indecisions and revisions also signify the ironic situations of modern people. What's more, the usual, common nature of his confession contrasts with the hyperbole by which he defines the confession.

4.4　Selected Readings

The Love Song of J. Alfred Prufrock

by T. S. Eliot

S'io credesse che mia risposta fosse

A persona che mai tornasse al mondo,

Questa fiamma staria senza piu scosse.

Ma perciocche giammai di questo fondo

Non torno vivo alcun, s'i'odo il vero,

Senza tema d'infamia ti rispondo.

Let us go then, you and I,

When the evening is spread out against the sky

Like a patient etherized upon a table;

Let us go, through certain half-deserted streets,

The muttering retreats

Of restless nights in one-night cheap hotels

And sawdust restaurants with oyster-shells:

Streets that follow like a tedious argument

Of insidious intent

To lead you to an overwhelming question…

Oh, do not ask, "What is it?"

Let us go and make our visit.

In the room the women come and go

Talking of Michelangelo.

The yellow fog that rubs its back upon the window-panes,

The yellow smoke that rubs its muzzle on the window-panes

Licked its tongue into the corners of the evening,

Lingered upon the pools that stand in drains,

Let fall upon its back the soot that falls from chimneys,

Slipped by the terrace, made a sudden leap,

And seeing that it was a soft October night,

Curled once about the house, and fell asleep.

And indeed there will be time

For the yellow smoke that slides along the street,

Rubbing its back upon the window-panes;

There will be time, there will be time

To prepare a face to meet the faces that you meet;

There will be time to murder and create,

And time for all the works and days of hands

That lift and drop a question on your plate;

Time for you and time for me,

And time yet for a hundred indecisions,

And for a hundred visions and revisions,

Before the taking of a toast and tea.

In the room the women come and go

Talking of Michelangelo.

And indeed there will be time

To wonder, "Do I dare?" and, "Do I dare?"

Time to turn back and descend the stair,

With a bald spot in the middle of my hair—

[They will say: "How his hair is growing thin!"]

My morning coat, my collar mounting firmly to the chin,

My necktie rich and modest, but asserted by a simple pin—

[They will say: "But how his arms and legs are thin!"]

Do I dare

Disturb the universe?

In a minute there is time

For decisions and revisions which a minute will reverse.

For I have known them all already, known them all—

Have known the evenings, mornings, afternoons,

I have measured out my life with coffee spoons;

I know the voices dying with a dying fall

Beneath the music from a farther room.

So how should I presume?

And I have known the eyes already, known them all—

The eyes that fix you in a formulated phrase,

And when I am formulated, sprawling on a pin,

When I am pinned and wriggling on the wall,

Then how should I begin

To spit out all the butt-ends of my days and ways?

And how should I presume?

And I have known the arms already, known them all—

Arms that are braceleted and white and bare

[But in the lamplight, downed with light brown hair!]

Is it perfume from a dress

That makes me so digress?

Arms that lie along a table, or wrap about a shawl.

And should I then presume?

And how should I begin?

......

Shall I say, I have gone at dusk through narrow streets

And watched the smoke that rises from the pipes

Of lonely men in shirt-sleeves, leaning out of windows? …

I should have been a pair of ragged claws

Scuttling across the floors of silent seas.

......

And the afternoon, the evening, sleeps so peacefully!

Smoothed by long fingers,

Asleep… tired… or it malingers,

Stretched on the floor, here beside you and me.

Should I, after tea and cakes and ices,

Have the strength to force the moment to its crisis?

But though I have wept and fasted, wept and prayed,

Though I have seen my head [grown slightly bald] brought in upon a platter,

I am no prophet—and here's no great matter;

I have seen the moment of my greatness flicker,

And I have seen the eternal Footman hold my coat, and snicker,

And in short, I was afraid.

And would it have been worth it, after all,

After the cups, the marmalade, the tea,

Among the porcelain, among some talk of you and me,

Would it have been worthwhile,

To have bitten off the matter with a smile,

To have squeezed the universe into a ball

To roll it toward some overwhelming question,

To say: "I am Lazarus, come from the dead,

Come back to tell you all, I shall tell you all"—

If one, settling a pillow by her head,

Should say: "That is not what I meant at all.

That is not it, at all."

And would it have been worth it, after all,

Would it have been worthwhile,

After the sunsets and the dooryards and the sprinkled streets,

After the novels, after the teacups, after the skirts that trail along the floor—

And this, and so much more?—

It is impossible to say just what I mean!

But as if a magic lantern threw the nerves in patterns on a screen:

Would it have been worth while

If one, settling a pillow or throwing off a shawl,

And turning toward the window, should say:

"That is not it at all,

That is not what I meant, at all."

......

No! I am not Prince Hamlet, nor was meant to be;

Am an attendant lord, one that will do

To swell a progress, start a scene or two,

Advise the prince; no doubt, an easy tool,

Deferential, glad to be of use,

Politic, cautious, and meticulous;

Full of high sentence, but a bit obtuse;

At times, indeed, almost ridiculous—

Almost, at times, the Fool.

I grow old... I grow old...

I shall wear the bottoms of my trousers rolled.

Shall I part my hair behind? Do I dare to eat a peach?

I shall wear white flannel trousers, and walk upon the beach.

I have heard the mermaids singing, each to each.

I do not think that they will sing to me.

I have seen them riding seaward on the waves

Combing the white hair of the waves blown back

When the wind blows the water white and black.

We have lingered in the chambers of the sea

By sea-girls wreathed with seaweed red and brown

Till human voices wake us, and we drown.

Questions for discussion:

1. Who is the main character in "The Love Song of J. Alfred Prufrock"? How do you understand the relationship between "you" and "I" in this poem?

2. Can you see any ironic elements in this poem?

3. How does the imagery of the first fourteen lines of the poem create its psychological and emotional atmosphere?

4. How do you understand Eliot's attitudes towards "modern secularism" as seen in "*The Love Song of J. Alfred Prufrock*"?

5. Analyze the cultural allusions in this poem.

4.5　Appreciation of Selected Readings

正如前文所言，《普鲁弗洛克情歌》(*The Love Song of J. Alfred Prufrock*) 是一篇以戏剧独白形式展开的奇特情诗，也是现代主义诗人 T.S.艾略特早期创作的重要诗作。诗人通过独白展示主人公的经历，并间接描述了一个犹豫彷徨、有些过于敏感和怯懦，又期望有所迁延的生动人物。这个人物一方面害怕生命白白溜走，另一方面又对事实无可奈何。

诗人 T. S.艾略特给我们展示了一幅 20 世纪西方社会生活中的荒原画面，人们颓废、无力，社会弥漫着一种病态。诗中，"你"被"我"（诗歌中的独白 Prufrock）邀请一起去参加活动，虽然"你"在诗歌中出现的次数不多，但却见证了普鲁弗洛克（Prufrock）内心的挣扎、迷茫和痛苦。诗人将黄昏时蔓延在天边的暮色比喻成弥留的病人，在如此悲凉的背景渲染之中，独白者寻求着问题（"an overwhelming question"）的答案，这是一个"重大的问题"。诗歌结尾，"你"和"我"重新变为"我们"，犹如分裂的人物又融为一体，而"我们"在现实与理想的撕扯、挣扎中最终湮灭。在了解普鲁弗洛克的世界后，我们似乎才能理解普鲁弗洛克的世界——在诗中被揭示为一个无意义的、半明半暗的世界，一个被麻痹的梦境。苦苦挣扎的普鲁弗洛克最终放弃反抗，接受了"死亡"。诗歌主人翁的怯懦、逃避与痛苦映射了 20 世纪初西方现代中社会的衰败、无序现状和都市生活中的人们萎靡不振的心灵状态，它象征了一个失去信念的世界，一颗对生活意义失去理解的心和对任何事物都失去了该有的创造能力的世界。整首诗歌晦涩难懂，T. S.艾略特认为这是不可避免的，因为当今（20 世纪）社会和个人生活十分复杂多变，不可捉摸。

自 20 世纪以来，西方社会不乏有人将眼光投向东方，试图寻找将人们从现代文明背后隐藏的种种危机中解救出来的良药秘方，诗人 T. S.艾略特也曾到访过中国。作为中国的青年读者，我们物质丰富、精神充实，是引时代风气之先的一股强大力量。我们应该庆幸习近平新时代社会主义核心价值观为中国大学生指明了道路，我们应当以正确的价值观为引领，积极向上，努力生长。

4.6   Supplementary Reading

My Last Duchess

by Robert Browning

That's my last Duchess painted on the wall,

Looking as if she were alive. I call

That piece a wonder, now; Fra Pandolf's hands

Worked busily a day, and there she stands.

Will't please you sit and look at her? I said

'Fra Pandolf' by design, for never read

Strangers like you that pictured countenance,

The depth and passion of its earnest glance,

But to myself they turned (since none puts by

The curtain I have drawn for you, but I)

And seemed as they would ask me, if they durst,

How such a glance came there; so, not the first

Are you to turn and ask thus. Sir, 'twas not

Her husband's presence only, called that spot

Of joy into the Duchess' cheek; perhaps

Fra Pandolf chanced to say, 'Her mantle laps

Over my lady's wrist too much,' or 'Paint

Must never hope to reproduce the faint

Half-flush that dies along her throat:' Such stuff

Was courtesy, she thought, and cause enough

For calling up that spot of joy. She had

A heart—how shall I say?— too soon made glad,

Too easily impressed; she liked whate'er

She looked on, and her looks went everywhere.

Sir, 'twas all one! My favour at her breast,

The dropping of the daylight in the West,

The bough of cherries some officious fool

Broke in the orchard for her, the white mule

She rode with round the terrace—all and each

Would draw from her alike the approving speech,

Or blush, at least. She thanked men—good! but thanked

Somehow—I know not how—as if she ranked

My gift of a nine-hundred-years-old name

With anybody's gift. Who'd stoop to blame

This sort of trifling? Even had you skill

In speech—which I have not—to make your will

Quite clear to such an one, and say, 'Just this

Or that in you disgusts me; here you miss,

Or there exceed the mark'—and if she let

Herself be lessoned so, nor plainly set

Her wits to yours, forsooth, and made excuse,

—E'en then would be some stooping; and I choose

Never to stoop. Oh, sir, she smiled, no doubt,

Whene'er I passed her; but who passed without

Much the same smile? This grew; I gave commands;

Then all smiles stopped together. There she stands

As if alive. Will't please you rise? We'll meet

The company below, then. I repeat,

The Count your master's known munificence

Is ample warrant that no just pretense

Of mine for dowry will be disallowed;

Though his fair daughter's self, as I avowed

At starting, is my object. Nay, we'll go

Together down, sir. Notice Neptune, though,

Taming a sea-horse, thought a rarity,

Which Claus of Innsbruck cast in bronze for me!

Drama

Unit 1   General Introduction to Drama

1.1   The Origin of Drama

"All the world is a stage; all the men and women merely players." —— By Shakespeare

"What is drama but life with the dull bits cut out." ——By Hitchcock

It is commonly holds that a drama is a story enacted onstage for a live audience. "Drama" comes from a Greek word "dran", meaning "thing done", "action", or "deed". Aristotle (384—322B.C.) is the first and still the single most important theorist of drama who called drama "imitated human action".

The earliest known plays were written around the fifth century B.C. They were produced for festivals to honor Dionysus, the god of wine and fertility. Typically, there are three stages of drama's development. First, ancient Greek drama witnessed the development both in comedy and tragedy in 6 B.C. The best remembered are those great tragedies like *Prometheus Bound* by Aeschylus (525—456B.C.), *Oedipus the King* by Sophocles (496—406B.C.) and *Medea* by Electra / Euripides (484—406B.C.).Second, ancient Roman drama was comedy. Third, mid-century drama came into being by its basis on the rituals for the birth of Jesus and His resurrection, thus it's religious. And it falls into three kinds, mystery play, miracle play and morality play. One of the great flowering of drama in England occurred in the 16th and 17th centuries. Many of these plays were written in verse, particularly iambic pentameter. In addition to Shakespeare, such authors as Christopher Marlowe, Thomas Middleton, and Ben Jonson were prominent playwrights during this period. As in the medieval period, historical plays celebrated the lives of past kings, English playwrights enhanced the image of the Tudor monarchy by drawing some of their storylines from Greek mythology and Roman mythology or from the plays of eminent Roman playwrights.

Aristotle categorized drama into six types in his "Poetics" in order of importance as he views them: plot, character, thought, diction, music and spectacle. This is the first surviving example of dramatic theory. J.M. Manly saw three necessary elements in drama: 1) a story; 2) told in action; 3) by actors who impersonate the characters of the story. In English, the word play or game was the standard term for dramas until William Shakespeare's time.

Drama can be classified into several groups: tragedy, comedy, tragicomedy, melodrama, problem play and farce.

Tragedy describes the fall from prosperity to adversity of a person of significance, or a hero, because he has transgressed against the great moral principles which govern the universe. Shakespeare's four great tragedies reflect the evil and the corruption of man's heart by evil. *Hamlet* puts the fighting against the outside evil onstage; *Othello* reveals an outward evil that causes a man's fall; *King Lear* centers on man's mistakes setting free the evils and *Macbeth* exposes an outward evil that destroys a hero.

1.2 The Elements of Drama

The basic elements of drama involve setting, act, scene, conflict, dialogue, structure and theme.

Aristotle was one of the first to write about drama and describe its three segments: beginning, middle, and end. Over time, dramas evolved, the Roman poet, Horace advocated for five acts, and many centuries later, a German playwright, Gustav Freytag, developed the five acts structure commonly used today, which expands the classical divisions. A well built tragedy, for example, will commonly show five divisions, each representing a phase of the dramatic conflicts. Shakespearean plays especially are known for following this structure. Act 1: The Exposition. The audience learns the setting (Time/Place), characters are developed, and a conflict is introduced. Act 2: Rising Action. The action of this act leads the audience to the climax. It is common for complications to arise, or for the protagonist to encounter obstacles. Act 3: The Climax. This is the turning point of the play. The climax is characterized by the highest amount of suspense. Act 4: Falling Action. The opposite of Rising Action, in the Falling Action the story is coming to an end, and any unknown details or plot twists are revealed and wrapped up. Act 5: Denouement or Resolution. This is the final outcome of the drama. Here the authors tone about his or her subject matter is revealed, and sometimes a moral or lesson is learned.

Unit 2　Conflict in Drama: *King Lear*

2.1　Elements of Drama: Conflict

Conflict refers to the struggle that comes from the interplay of two or more opposing forces in the play. They are indispensable in drama because it is the dramatic conflicts that hold the audience's heartstrings and get them emotionally or ideologically involved. As the saying goes, there is no drama without conflict. Conflict involves a struggle between two opposing forces, usually a protagonist and an antagonist. There are different kinds of conflicts in drama: internal conflict, external conflict, core conflict. It is often the case that different kinds of conflicts combine to work out the destiny of the protagonist, as in Shakespeare's *King Lear*. Considering man's basic relationship with the world around his and within him, there are four kinds of conflicts that a person, usually a protagonist, may be involved in: the conflict with nature, the conflict with another person, the conflict with society, the conflict with himself. Hamlet's internal conflict is the main driver in William Shakespeare's play Hamlet." It decides his tragic downfall. He reveals his state of mind in the following lines from Act 3, Scene I of the play:

"To be, or not to be—that is the question:

Whether 'tis nobler in the mind to suffer

The slings and arrows of outrageous fortune

Or to take arms against a sea of troubles

And by opposing end them. To die, to sleep…"

The conflict here is that Hamlet wants to kill his father's murderer, Claudius, but he also looks for proof to justify his action. In the same play, we find Hamlet also engaged in an external conflict with his uncle Claudius.

In ancient Greek drama, there seems to be another kind of conflict, a struggle with Fate or Destiny. However, such a conflict is usually embodied in one or more of the aforesaid conflicts.

2.2   William Shakespeare and His Achievements

Shakespeare was hailed by Ben Jonson in a now-famous quote as "not of an age, but for all time". The First Folio, was published in 1623, a posthumous collected edition of Shakespeare's dramatic works that included all but two of his plays. Most of his known plays were produced between 1589 and 1613. His early plays were primarily comedies and histories and are regarded as some of the best work produced in these genres. He then wrote mainly tragedies until 1608, among them *Hamlet*, *Romeo* and *Juliet*, *Othello*, *King Lear*, and *Macbeth*, all considered to be among the finest works in the English language. In the last phase of his life, he wrote tragicomedies (also known as romances) and collaborated with other playwrights. Shakespeare's works have made a lasting impression on later theatre and literature. In particular, he expanded the dramatic potential of characterization, plot, language, and genre. Until *Romeo and Juliet*, for example, romance had not been viewed as a worthy topic for tragedy. **Soliloquies** had been used mainly to convey information about characters or events, but Shakespeare used them to explore characters' minds. What's more, in Shakespeare's day, English grammar, spelling, and pronunciation were less standardized than they are now, and his use of language helped shape modern English. It is no exaggeration to say that Shakespeare's influence extends far beyond his native England and the English language.

2.3   The Plots of the Drama

King Lear, a tragedy in five acts by William Shakespeare, was written in 1605 and published in a quarto edition in 1608.

It is a story of the ageing king of Britain, Lear, and his three daughters, Goneril, Regan, and Cordelia. The ageing King Lear decides to divide his kingdom among his three daughters, allotting each a portion in proportion to the eloquence of her declaration of love. When asked to prove their love for him in exchange for one third of his kingdom, Cordelia, the youngest daughter, who truly loves Lear, refuses to make an insincere speech to prove her love and thus is disinherited. Cordelia is banished soon. The two older sisters mock Lear and treated him badly by breaking their promise to support him. They send him out of their houses in a state of half-madness with only his most loyal servants to protect him. Meanwhile, the Earl of Gloucester's evil bastard son, Edmund, attempts to usurp his father and elder brother Edgar, plotting to kill his father and have loyal Edgar banished from their home.

So, the families appear to be loving and caring at first, but this could not be further from the truth. As the characters unfold, we find greed, betrayal, lust for power, and cruelty. In other words, they are anything but normal and caring.

King Lear is aided by the Earl of Kent, who, though banished from the kingdom for having supported Cordelia, has remained in Britain disguised as a loyal follower of the king. Cordelia, having married the king of France, is obliged to invade her native country with a French army in order to rescue her neglected father. She is brought to Lear, cares for him, and helps him regain his reason.

The end of the play ends in death everywhere. When defeated, Cordelia and her father are taken into custody. Regan dies after being poisoned by Goneril. Goneril stabs herself to death. Edgar reveals his true identity to his father, but the old man dies. Mortally wounded, Edmund becomes remorseful and countermands his order to hang Cordelia. But it is too late, and Cordelia dies. Lear, now a broken man, falls upon Cordelia and also dies.

Edgar kills his cruel half-brother in a duel. Goneril's husband, Albany, takes up the throne of Britain after the play's bloodbath concludes.

2.4　Selected Readings

King Lear
(Excepts)
Act I

SCENE I .
King Lear's palace.
Enter Kent, Gloucester, and Edmund
KENT
I thought the king had more affected the Duke
Of Albany than Cornwall.
GLOUCESTER

It did always seem so to us: but now, in

the division of the kingdom, it appears not which

of the dukes he values most; for equalities are

so weighed, that curiosity in neither can make

choice of either's moiety.

KENT

Is not this your son, my lord?

GLOUCESTER

His breeding, sir, hath been at my charge: I

have so often blushed to acknowledge him, that now I

am brazed to it.

KENT

I cannot conceive you.

GLOUCESTER

Sir, this young fellow's mother could:

whereupon she grew round-wombed, and had, indeed, sir, a

son for her cradle ere she had a husband for her

bed. Do you smell a fault?

KENT

I cannot wish the fault undone, the issue of

it being so proper.

GLOUCESTER

But I have, sir, a son by order of law, some

year elder than this, who yet is no dearer in my

account:though this knave came something saucily into

the world before he was sent for, yet was his

mother fair; there was good sport at his making, and

the whoreson must be acknowledged.

Do you know this noble gentleman, Edmund?

EDMUND

[comes fonward] No, my lord.

GLOUCESTER

My lord of Kent, remember him hereafter as

my honourable friend.

EDMUND

My services to your lordship.

KENT

I must love you, and sue to know you better.

EDMUND

Sir, I shall study deserving.

GLOUCESTER

He hath been out nine years, and away he

shall again. Sound a sonnet.

The king is coming.

Enter one bearing a coronet, then Lear; then the Albany and Cornwall, Goneril,
kegan.

KING LEAR

Attend the lords of France and Burgundy, Gloucester.

GLOUCESTER

I shall, my liege.

Exeunt [Gloucester and Edmund].

KING LEAR

Meantime we shall express our darker purpose.

Give me the map there. Know that we have divided

in three our kingdom: and 'tis our fast intent

To shake all cares and business from our age,

Conferring them on younger strengths while we

unburthened crawl toward death.

Our son of Cornwall,

And you, our no less loving son of Albany,

We have this hour a constant will to publish

our daughters' several dowers, that future strife

may be prevented now. The princes, France and Burgundy,

Great rivals in our youngest daughter's love,

Long in our court have made their amorous sojourn,

And here are to be answered. Tell me, my daughters,

Since now we will divest us both of rule,

Interest of territory, cares of state,

Which of you shall we say doth love us most?

That we our largest bounty may extend

Where nature doth with merit challenge. Goneril,

Our eldest-born, speak first.

GONERIL

Sir, I love you more than words can wield the matter;

Dearer than eye-sight, space, and liberty;

Beyond what can be valued, rich or rare;

No less than life, with grace, health, beauty, honour;

As much as child e'er loved, or father found;

A love that makes breath poor, and speech unable.

Beyond all manner of so much I love you.

CORDELIA

What shall Cordelia do?

Love, and be silent.

LEAR

Of all these bounds, even from this line to this,

With shadowy forests and with champains riched,

With plenteous rivers and wide-skirted meads,

We make thee lady. To thine and Albany's issue

Be this perpetual. What says our second daughter,

Our dearest Regan, wife to Cornwall? Speak.

REGAN

Sir, I am

of the self-same metal that my sister is,

And prize me at her worth. In my true heart

I find she names my very deed of love;

Only she comes too short: that I profess

Myself an enemy to all other joys,

Which the most precious square of sense possesses;

And find I am alone felicitate

In your dear highness' love.

CORDELIA

Then poor Cordelia!

And yet not so; since, I am sure, my love's

More richer than my tongue.

KING LEAR

To thee and thine hereditary ever

Remain this ample third of our fair kingdom,

No less in space, validity, and pleasure,

Than that conferred on Goneril. Now, our joy,

Although the last, not least; to whose young love

The vines of France and milk of Burgundy

Strive to be interest; what can you say to draw

A third more opulent than your sisters? Speak.

CORDELIA

Nothing, my lord.

KING LEAR

Nothing?

CORDELIA

Nothing.

KING LEAR

Nothing will come of nothing. Speak again.

CORDELIA

Unhappy that I am, I cannot heave

My heart into my mouth. I love your majesty

According to my bond; nor more nor less.

KING LEAR

How, how, Cordelia? Mend your speech a little,

Lest it may mar your fortunes.

CORDELIA

Good my lord,

You have begot me, bred me, loved me, I

Return those duties back as are right fit,

Obey you, love you, and most honour you.

Why have my sisters husbands, if they say

They love you all? Haply, when I shall wed,

That lord whose hand must take my plight shall carry

Half my love with him, half my care and duty:

Sure, I shall never marry like my sisters,

To love my father all.

KING LEAR

But goes thy heart with this?

CORDELIA

Ay, good my lord.

KING LEAR

So young, and so untender?

CORDELIA

So young, my lord, and true.

KING LEAR

Let it be so! Thy truth, then, be thy dower!

For, by the sacred radiance of the sun,

The mysteries of Hecate, and the night;

By all the operation of the orbs

From whom we do exist, and cease to be;

Here I disclaim all my paternal care,

Propinquity and property of blood,

And as a stranger to my heart and me

Hold thee, from this, forever. The barbarous Scythian,

Or he that makes his generation messes

To gorge his appetite, shall to my bosom

Be as well neighboured, pitied, and relieved,

As thou my sometime daughter.

KENT

Good my liege,

KING LEAR

Peace, Kent!

Come not between the dragon and his wrath.

I loved her most, and thought to set my rest

On her kind nursery. Hence, and avoid my sight!

So be my grave my peace, as here I give

Her father's heart from her! Call France! Who stirs?

Call Burgundy. Cornwall and Albany,

With my two daughters' dowers digest this third:

Let pride, which she calls plainness, marry her.

I do invest you jointly with my power,

Pre-eminence, and all the large effects

That troop with majesty. Ourself, by monthly course,

With reservation of an hundred knights,

By you to be sustained, shall our abode

Make with you by due turns. Only we still retain

The name, and all the additions to a king. The sway,

Revenue, execution of the rest,

Beloved sons, be yours: which to confirm,

This coronet part betwixt you.

KENT

Royal Lear,

Whom I have ever honoured as my king,

Loved as my father, as my master followed,

As my great patron thought on in my prayers.

KING LEAR

The bow is bent and drawn, make from the shaft.

KENT

Let it fall rather, though the fork invade

The region of my heart! Be Kent unmannerly,

When Lear is mad. What wouldst thou do, old man?

Think'st thou that duty shall have dread to speak,

When power to flattery bows? To plainness honour's bound,

When majesty falls to folly. Reverse thy doom;

And, in thy best consideration, check

This hideous rashness. Answer my life my judgment,

Thy youngest daughter does not love thee least,

Nor are those empty-hearted whose low sound

Reverbs no hollowness.

KING LEAR

Kent, on thy life, no more!

KENT

My life I never held but as a pawn

To wage against thy enemies; nor fear to lose it,

Thy safety being the motive.

KING LEAR

Out of my sight!

KENT

See better, Lear, and let me still remain

The true blank of thine eye.

KING LEAR

Now, by Apollo.

KENT

Now, by Apollo, king,

Thou swear'st thy gods in vain.

KING LEAR

O, vassal! Miscreant!

Laying his hand on his sword.

ALBANY CORNWALL

Corn. Dear sir, forbear!

KENT

Kill thy physician, and the fee bestow

Upon thy foul disease. Revoke thy gift;

Or, whilst I can vent clamour from my throat,

I'll tell thee thou dost evil.

KING LEAR

Hear me, recreant!

On thine allegiance, hear me!

Since thou hast sought to make us break our vow,

Which we durst never yet, and with strained pride

To come between our sentence and our power,

Which nor our nature nor our place can bear,

Our potency made good, take thy reward.

Five days we do allot thee, for provision

To shield thee from diseases of the world,

And on the sixth to turn thy hated back

Upon our kingdom. If, on the tenth day following,

Thy banished trunk be found in our dominions,

The moment is thy death. Away! by Jupiter,

This shall not be revoked.

KENT

Fare thee well, king. Since thus thou wilt appear,

Freedom lives hence, and banishment is here.

[To Cordelia]

The gods to their dear shelter take thee, maid,

That justly think'st, and hast most rightly said!

[To Regan and Goneril]

And your large speeches may your deeds approve,

That good effects may spring from words of love.

Thus Kent, O princes, bids you all adieu;

He'll shape his old course in a country new.

Exit

Flourish. Enter Gloucester, with France and Burgundy, Attendants.

GLOUCESTER

Here's France and Burgundy, my noble lord.

KING LEAR

My lord of Burgundy.

We first address towards you, who with this king

Hath rivalled for our daughter. What, in the least,

Will you require in present dower with her,

Or cease your quest of love?

BURGUNDY

Most royal majesty,

I crave no more than hath your highness offered,

Nor will you tender less.

KING LEAR

Right noble Burgundy,

When she was dear to us, we did hold her so;

But now her price is fall'n. Sir, there she stands:

If aught within that little seeming substance,

Or all of it, with our displeasure pieced,

And nothing more, may fitly like your Grace,

She's there, and she is yours.

BURGUNDY

I know no answer.

KING LEAR

Will you, with those infirmities she owes,

Unfriended, new-adopted to our hate,

Dower'd with our curse, and strangered with our oath,

Take her, or leave her?

BURGUNDY

Pardon me, royal sir;

Election makes not up on such conditions.

KING LEAR

Then leave her, sir; for, by the power that made me,

I tell you all her wealth.

[To France]

For you, great king,

I would not from your love make such a stray,

To match you where I hate; therefore beseech you

To avert your liking a more worthier way

Than on a wretch whom nature is ashamed

Almost to acknowledge hers.

KING OF FRANCE

This is most strange,

That she, that even but now was your best object,

The argument of your praise, balm of your age,

Most best, most dearest, should in this trice of time

Commit a thing so monstrous, to dismantle

So many folds of favour. Sure, her offence

Must be of such unnatural degree,

That monsters it, or your fore-vouched affection

Fall'n into taint: which to believe of her,

Must be a faith that reason without miracle

Could never plant in me.

CORDELIA

I yet beseech your majesty,

If for I want that glib and oily art,

To speak and purpose not, since what I well intend,

I'll do't before I speak,—that you make known

It is no vicious blot, murder, or foulness,

No unchaste action or dishonoured step,

That hath deprived me of your grace and favour;

But even for want of that for which I am richer,

A still-soliciting eye, and such a tongue

As I am glad I have not, though not to have it

Hath lost me in your liking.

KING LEAR

Better thou

Hadst not been born than not to have pleased me better.

KING OF FRANCE

Is it but this,—a tardiness in nature

Which often leaves the history unspoke

That it intends to do? My lord of Burgundy,

What say you to the lady? Love's not love

When it is mingled with regards that stand

Aloof from the entire point. Will you have her?

She is herself a dowry.

BURGUNDY

Royal Lear,

Give but that portion which yourself proposed,

And here I take Cordelia by the hand,

Duchess of Burgundy.

KING LEAR

Nothing! I have sworn; I am firm.

BURGUNDY

I am sorry, then, you have so lost a father

That you must lose a husband.

CORDELIA

Peace be with Burgundy!

Since that respects of fortune are his love,

I shall not be his wife.

KING OF FRANCE

Fairest Cordelia, that art most rich, being poor;

Most choice, forsaken; and most loved, despised!

Thee and thy virtues here I seize upon:

Be it lawful I take up what's cast away.

Gods, gods! 'tis strange that from their coldest neglect

My love should kindle to inflamed respect.

Thy dowerless daughter, king, thrown to my chance,

Is queen of us, of ours, and our fair France:

Not all the dukes of waterish Burgundy

Can buy this unprized precious maid of me.

Bid them farewell, Cordelia, though unkind:

Thou losest here, a better where to find.

KING LEAR

Thou hast her, France: let her be thine; for we

Have no such daughter, nor shall ever see

That face of hers again. Therefore be gone

Without our grace, our love, our benison.

Come, noble Burgundy.

Flourish. Exeunt Lear, Burgundy, [Cornwall, Albany, Gloucester, and Atcendants].

KING OF FRANCE

Bid farewell to your sisters.

CORDELIA

The jewels of our father, with washed eyes

Cordelia leaves you: I know you what you are;

And like a sister am most loath to call

Your faults as they are named. Use well our father:

To your professed bosoms I commit him

But yet, alas, stood I within his grace,

I would prefer him to a better place!

So, farewell to you both.

REGAN

Prescribe not us our duties.

GONERIL

Let your study

Be to content your lord, who hath received you

At fortune's alms.

You have obedience scanted,

And well are worth the want that you have wanted.

CORDELIA

Time shall unfold what plaited cunning hides:

Who cover faults, at last shame them derides.

Well may you prosper!

KING OF FRANCE

Come, my fair Cordelia.

Exeunt France and Cordelia

GONERIL

Sister, it is not a little I have to say of

What most nearly appertains to us both. I think

Our father will hence to-night.

REGAN

That's most certain, and with you; next month with us.

GONERIL

You see how full of changes his age is;

The observation we have made of it hath not

been little: he always loved our sister most;

and with what poor judgment he hath now cast her

off appears too grossly.

REGAN

'Tis the infirmity of his age; yet he hath

Ever but slenderly known himself.

GONERIL

The best and soundest of his time hath been

but rash; then must we look to receive from his age,

not alone the imperfections of long-engraffed

condition, but therewithal the unruly waywardness

that infirm and choleric years bring with them.

REGAN

Such unconstant starts are we like to have

From him as this of Kent's banishment.

GONERIL

There is further compliment of leave

Taking between France and him. Pray you, let's

Hit together. If our father carry authority

With such dispositions as he bears, this

Last surrender of his will but offend us.

REGAN

We shall further think on't.

GONERIL

We must do something, and i' the heat.

Exeunt

Questions for discussion:

1.　How can pride cause someone to make foolish decisions?

2.　Why is it important to think through a situation, rather than make rash decisions?

3.　What are the potential dangers of greed?

4.　Why is forgiveness so important?

2.5　Appreciation of Selected Readings

　　《李尔王》（*King Lear*）是莎士比亚"最伟大的作品、他戏剧中最好的一部"。该戏剧讲述年事已高的国王李尔即将退位之时，召集三位女儿分封国土的故事。他根据女儿们对他的赞美来决定分给他们的国土份额。两个大女儿（Goneril, Regan）表达了对父亲的无限热爱，小女儿（Cordelia）却沉默，拒绝回答。因此，老国王将全部国土和权力交给两个大女儿，并剥夺了小女儿的继承权，将她远嫁法兰西。梦想着悠闲任性地度过自己晚年生活的李尔王却在暴风雨之夜被女儿们赶到荒郊野外。整个剧本中，从国王到乞丐，从宫廷到荒野，从落难的暴怒到和解的温和，从残忍和悲惨到忠诚和善良，李尔王尝尽了人情冷暖，世态炎凉，最后饮恨而死。这是一出彻头彻尾的悲剧，小女儿率军救父，却被杀死，李尔王最终伤心地死在她身旁，让人感到彻底的悲凉。

　　《李尔王》（*King Lear*）创作于文艺复兴时期，正是英国社会从古代封建社会向近代资本主义社会的过渡阶段。戏剧中的李尔王因迷失于神圣至上的君主权力而变得专横、傲慢、暴躁、反复无常。权势给他带来的尊荣、自豪、自信，却迷失了他的本性，使得他丧失理智，幻想以让权分国来证明自己不当国王而做一个普通人也能同样或更加伟大，因而经受了痛苦的磨难。清醒之时，已无法挽回自己的错误。莎士比亚的作品正如一面镜子，将生活真实放大，深刻地反映了时代风貌和社会本质。

李尔王的小女儿考狄利娅在剧本中代表了人和人之间的和谐真诚、尊重人格、平等相待等的人文主义思想。但李尔的疯狂致死、考狄利娅的被害和葛罗斯特的流浪等结局，又为作品抹上了浓重的忧郁色调。可以说，《李尔王》不仅真实地反映了资本主义世界资本原始积累时期动荡不安的英国社会的面貌，也流露出作者对专制王权的批判和对人性的歌颂。《李尔王》的悲剧高度概括了人文主义理想与残酷现实之间矛盾的不可调和性。我们可以清醒地认识到李尔王因刚愎自用而付出了生命的代价，也给国家和人民带来了巨大的灾难。

当今世界文化、社会的交流日益频繁。日益走近世界舞台中心的中国正在为构建人类命运共同体贡献中国智慧和中国方案。当代中国大学生应该响应国家发展，积极"讲好中国故事"，这是我们的责任和使命。习近平在谈治国理政中特别强调家风的建设，认为"家是最小国，国是千万家。"天下之本在家。家风是一个家庭的精神内核，也是一个社会的价值缩影。莎士比亚悲剧《李尔王》集中体现了莎士比亚否定家长权威和"违逆天性"（"Filialing gratitude" from Act III, Scene 4）的戏剧主题，家风不正是李尔王乃至整个国家悲剧的根源。新时代我们应当更加积极地参与到讲家风，传承红色基因，营造文明和谐家庭，维护社会主义国家稳定的时代大潮之中。

2.6　Supplementary Reading

An Essay of Dramatic Poesy(Excepts)

by John Dryden

If your quarrel (said *Eugenius*) to those who now write, be grounded only upon your reverence to Antiquity, there is no man more ready to adore those great Greeks and Romans than I am: but on the other side, I cannot think so contemptibly of the Age I live in, or so dishonourably of my own Countrey, as not to judge we equal the Ancients in most kinds of Poesie, and in some surpass them; neither know I any reason why I may not be as zealous for the Reputation of our Age, as we find the Ancients themselves in reference to those who lived before them. For you hear your Horace saying:

Indignor quidquam reprehendi, non quia crassé Compositum, illepidève putetur, sed quia nuper.

And after,

Si meliora dies, ut vina, poemata reddit, Scire velim pretium chartis quotus arroget annus?

But I see I am ingaging in a wide dispute, where the arguments are not like to reach close on either side; for Poesie is of so large extent, and so many both of the Ancients and Moderns have done well in all kinds of it, that, in citing one against the other, we shall take up more time this Evening, than each mans occasions will allow him: therefore I would ask Crites to what part of Poesie he would confine his Arguments, and whether he would defend the general cause of the Ancients against the Moderns, or oppose any Age of the Moderns against this of ours?

Crites a little while considering upon this Demand, told *Eugenius* he approv'd his Propositions, and, if he pleased, he would limit their Dispute to *Dramatique Poesie*; in which he thought it not difficult to prove, either that the Antients were superiour to the Moderns, or the last Age to this of ours.

Eugenius was somewhat surpriz'd, when he heard *Crites* make choice of that Subject; For ought I see, said he, I have undertaken a harder Province than I imagin'd; for though I never judg'd the Plays of the Greek or Roman Poets comparable to ours; yet on the other side those we now see acted, come short of many which were written in the last Age: but my comfort is if we are orecome, it will be only by our own Countreymen: and if we yield to them in this one part of Poesie, we more surpass them in all the other; for in the Epique or Lyrique way it will be hard for them to show us one such amongst them, as we have many now living, or who lately were so. They can produce nothing so courtly writ, or which expresses so much the Conversation of a Gentleman, as Sir John Suckling; nothing so even, sweet, and flowing as *Mr. Waller*; nothing so Majestique, so correct as *Sir John Denham*; nothing so elevated, so copious, and full of spirit, as *Mr Cowley*; as for the Italian, French, and Spanish Plays, I can make it evident that those who now write, surpass them; and that the Drama is wholly ours.

All of them were thus far of *Eugenius* his opinion, that the sweetness of English

Verse was never understood or practis'd by our Fathers; even Crites himself did not much oppose it: and every one was willing to acknowledge how much our Poesie is improv'd, by the happiness of some Writers yet living; who first taught us to mould our thoughts into easie and significant words; to retrench the superfluities of expression, and to make our Rime so properly a part of the Verse, that it should never mis-lead the sence, but it self be led and govern'd by it. Eugenius was going to continue this Discourse, when Lisideius told him it was necessary, before they proceeded further, to take a standing measure of their Controversie; for how was it possible to be decided who writ the best Plays, before we know what a Play should be? but, this once agreed on by both Parties, each might have recourse to it, either to prove his own advantages, or discover the failings of his Adversary.

He had no sooner said this, but all desir'd the favour of him to give the definition of a Play; and they were the more importunate, because neither Aristotle, nor Horace, nor any other, who writ of that Subject, had ever done it.

Unit 3　Dialogue in Drama: *Pygmalion*

3.1　Elements of Drama: Dialogue

The term "dialogue" was used by Plato to describe Socratic dialectic works, gradually it tends to serve many functions such as adding context to a narrative, establishing voice and tone, or setting forth conflict. Drama is special genre of literature, in which the words are mainly dialogue. People-talking is seen as the basic representative action. The dialogues of the characters, when talking to one another, are instrumental in promoting and advancing the interplay of ideas and the revelation of the personalities of the characters.

As a literary device, dialogue can be utilized in almost any form of literature. Since plays are dramatic literary works to be performed on stage, they often rely almost exclusively on dialogue between characters as a means of presenting different points of view, revealing conflict in a story, and moving plots forward. The reason is that there is no narrator in drama to tell the audience about all these information. Besides, dialogue is more subtle in conveying the inner feelings and intentions of a character beyond their surface words of communication, thus allowing characters to engage in conflict and creating authenticity for the audience.

Sometimes the dramatist uses a soliloquy to present what is going on in the mind of the characters in order for the audience to understand them better. The most famous soliloquy is "To be or not to be" in *Hamlet*.

3.2 George Bernard Shaw and His Achievements

George Bernard Shaw was an Irish comic dramatist, literary critic, and socialist spokesman. He was born in 1856 in Dublin, in a lower-middle class family of Scottish-Protestant ancestry. His father was a failed corn-merchant, with a drinking problem and a squint; his mother was the daughter of an impoverished landowner. Despite his failure as a novelist in the 1880s, Shaw found himself during this decade. Shaw turned to literature and began his career by writing theatre, criticism, music and novels. From 1885 to 1911, Shaw became involved in progressive politics. 1895 onwards, Shaw worked as Theatre Critic and wrote drama criticism for the "Saturday Review". Shaw's early plays include *Widower's Houses* (1891) and *Mrs. Warren's Profession*. His first success came with the publication of *Arms and the Man* in 1894. Shaw's other important plays include *Caesar and Cleopatra* (1899), *Major Barbara* (1905), *Pygmalion* (1914). The outbreak of war in 1914 changed Shaw's life. Shaw's popularity declined significantly. After the war, Shaw found his dramatic voice again and rebuilt his reputation. He was accepted once again with the publication of *Saint Joan* in 1923. In 1925 he was awarded the Nobel Prize for Literature. George Bernard Shaw wrote masterpieces, which brought praiseworthy changes into the world of literature.

George Bernard Shaw died on November 2, 1950 in Ayot St. Lawrence, Hertfordshire, at the age of 94.

3.3 The Plots of the Drama

People-talking is seen as the basic representative action. The dialogues of the characters in this play are used as a means of revealing the personalities of the characters and the conflicts in a story, and moving plots forward.

Pygmalion, a romance in five acts, was first premiered in German in 1913 in Vienna and performed in England in 1914. The play, possibly Shaw's comedic masterpiece based on the Grecian myth of the same name, is a humane comedy about love and the English class system. In this play, George. Bernard Shaw beautifully presents his social assumption of having a status based on the manners and sophistication of accent instead of the hereditary ownership and ethnic nobility. The play was inspired in making various adaptations both on-stage as well as in movies. It was first filmed in 1938 and then as a musical film version released in 1964 under the name *My Fair Lady*. Both films won applause from the audiences.

The play shows Professor Higgins' meeting Colonel Pickering in the Covent Garden during a rainy night. Both are interested in linguistics; the first as a phonetician and the second as an expert of an Indian, especially Sanskrit dialects and language. Henry Higgins accepts a bet that simply by changing the speech of a Cockney flower girl he will be able, in six months, to pass her off as a lady.

Higgins takes Eliza Doolittle with him to Wimpole Street to train her. Eliza undergoes grueling training. She also takes some interest, seeing phonetic training to better her career prospects. Higgins asks Eliza to change her personality. After a few months and a lot of hard work by Eliza, Higgins succeeds in making her speak fluently in the accent spoken by the nobility of England. The scene, in which Eliza Doolittle appears in high society when she has acquired a correct accent but no notion of polite conversation, is one of the funniest in English drama.

When she successfully "passes" in high society—having in the process become a lovely young woman of sensitivity and taste—Higgins dismisses her abruptly as a successfully completed experiment. Eliza, who now belongs neither to the upper class, whose mannerisms and speech she has learned, nor to the lower class, from which she came, rejects his dehumanizing attitude. Feeling hurt "at heart". Eliza gets furious at this neglect, and throws her slipper at Higgins as he asks her to marry somebody high class, a remark which hurts her the most after which she returns his jewelry.

The next morning when Professor Higgins gets up, he sees Eliza absent. On inquiry, he finds that she has fled. Panicked, he reaches his mother, asking about her whereabouts. Although she is with her, she tells her not to come downstairs. Mrs. Higgins speaks to Higgins and Pickering and tells them that she had the right to leave the house and not want to live with him because of the way he has treated her and taunts for playing with the emotions of the girl.

Higgins responds to her stating that he is cold to everyone in spite of their class and treats everyone the same regardless of their good or bad manners. Eliza says that if she can't get kindness from him then at least she needs her freedom. Alongside, she will start teaching phonetics, stealing all his methods. The professor starts showering praise on her for the woman she has become and she is not that silly flower girl anymore.

The play ends when Eliza leaves the room saying that she will not do his chores anymore and ask him to do himself and Higgins alone in the room, thinking she'll do as he has asked her.

3.4　Selected Readings

Pygmalion

(Excepts)

ACT 1

Covent Garden at 11.15 p.m. Torrents of heavy summer rain. Cab whistles blowing frantically in all directions. Pedestrians running for shelter into the market and under the portico of St. Paul's Church, where there are already several people, among them a lady and her daughter in evening dress. They are all peering out gloomily at the rain, except one man with his back turned to the rest, who seems wholly preoccupied with a notebook in which he is writing busily.

The church clock strikes the first quarter.

THE DAUGHTER [in the space between the central pillars, close to the one on her left] I'm getting chilled to the bone. What can Freddy be doing all this time? He's been gone twenty minutes.

THE MOTHER [on her daughter's right] Not so long. But he ought to have got us a cab by this.

A BYSTANDER [on the lady's right] He won't get no cab not until half-past eleven, missus, when they come back after dropping their theatre fares.

THE MOTHER. But we must have a cab. We can't stand here until half-past eleven. It's too bad.

THE BYSTANDER. Well, it ain't my fault, missus.

THE DAUGHTER. If Freddy had a bit of gumption, he would have got one at the theatre door.

THE MOTHER. What could he have done, poor boy?

THE DAUGHTER. Other people got cabs. Why couldn't he?

Freddy rushes in out of the rain from the Southampton Street side, and comes between them closing a dripping umbrella. He is a young man of twenty, in evening dress, very wet around the ankles.

THE DAUGHTER. Well, haven't you got a cab?

FREDDY. There's not one to be had for love or money.

THE MOTHER. Oh, Freddy, there must be one. You can't have tried.

THE DAUGHTER. It's too tiresome. Do you expect us to go and get one ourselves?

FREDDY. I tell you they're all engaged. The rain was so sudden: nobody was prepared; and everybody had to take a cab. I've been to Charing Cross one way and nearly to Ludgate Circus the other; and they were all engaged.

THE MOTHER. Did you try Trafalgar Square?

FREDDY. There wasn't one at Trafalgar Square.

THE DAUGHTER. Did you try?

FREDDY. I tried as far as Charing Cross Station. Did you expect me to walk to Hammersmith?

THE DAUGHTER. You haven't tried at all.

THE MOTHER. You really are very helpless, Freddy. Go again; and don't come back until you have found a cab.

FREDDY. I shall simply get soaked for nothing.

THE DAUGHTER. And what about us? Are we to stay here all night in this draught, with next to nothing on. You selfish pig!

FREDDY. Oh, very well: I'll go, I'll go. [He opens his umbrella and dashes off Strandwards, but comes into collision with a flower girl, who is hurrying in for shelter, knocking her basket out of her hands. A blinding flash of lightning, followed instantly by a rattling peal of thunder, orchestrates the incident]

THE FLOWER GIRL. Nah then, Freddy: look wh' y' gow in, deah.

FREDDY. Sorry [he rushes off].

THE FLOWER GIRL [picking up her scattered flowers and replacing them in the basket] There's menners f' yer! Te-oo banches o voylets trod into the mad. [She sits down on the plinth of the column, sorting her flowers, on the lady's right. She is not at all an attractive person. She is perhaps eighteen, perhaps twenty, hardly older. She wears a little sailor hat of black straw that has long been exposed to the dust and soot of London and has seldom if ever been brushed. Her hair needs washing rather badly: its mousy color can hardly be natural. She wears a shoddy black coat that reaches nearly to her knees and is shaped to her waist. She has a brown skirt with a coarse apron. Her boots are much the worse for wear. She is no doubt as clean as she can afford to be; but compared to the ladies she is very dirty. Her features are no worse than theirs; but their condition leaves something to be desired; and she needs the services of a dentist].

THE MOTHER. How do you know that my son's name is Freddy, pray?

THE FLOWER GIRL. Ow, eez ye-ooa san, is e? Wal, fewd dan y' de-ooty bawmz a mather should, eed now bettern to spawl a pore gel's flahrzn than ran awy atbaht pyin. Will ye-oo py me f'them? [Here, with apologies, this desperate attempt to represent her dialect without a phonetic alphabet must be abandoned as unintelligible outside London.]

THE DAUGHTER. Do nothing of the sort, mother. The idea!

THE MOTHER. Please allow me, Clara. Have you any pennies?

THE DAUGHTER. No. I've nothing smaller than sixpence.

THE FLOWER GIRL [hopefully] I can give you change for a tanner, kind lady.

THE MOTHER [to Clara] Give it to me. [Clara parts reluctantly]. Now [to the girl] This is for your flowers.

THE FLOWER GIRL. Thank you kindly, lady.

THE DAUGHTER. Make her give you the change. These things are only a penny a bunch.

THE MOTHER. Do hold your tongue, Clara. [To the girl]. You can keep the change.

THE FLOWER GIRL. Oh, thank you, lady.

THE MOTHER. Now tell me how you know that young gentleman's name.

THE FLOWER GIRL. I didn't.

THE MOTHER. I heard you call him by it. Don't try to deceive me.

THE FLOWER GIRL [protesting] Who's trying to deceive you? I called him Freddy or Charlie same as you might yourself if you was talking to a stranger and wished to be pleasant. [She sits down beside her basket].

THE DAUGHTER. Sixpence thrown away! Really, mamma, you might have spared Freddy that. [She retreats in disgust behind the pillar].

An elderly gentleman of the amiable military type rushes into shelter, and closes a dripping umbrella. He is in the same plight as Freddy, very wet about the ankles. He is in evening dress, with a light overcoat. He takes the place left vacant by the daughter's retirement.

THE GENTLEMAN. Phew!

THE MOTHER [to the gentleman] Oh, sir, is there any sign of its stopping?

THE GENTLEMAN. I'm afraid not. It started worse than ever about two minutes ago. [He goes to the plinth beside the flower girl; puts up his foot on it; and stoops to turn down his trouser ends].

THE MOTHER. Oh, dear! [She retires sadly and joins her daughter].

THE FLOWER GIRL [taking advantage of the military gentleman's proximity to establish friendly relations with him]. If it's worse it's a sign it's nearly over. So cheer up, Captain; and buy a flower off a poor girl.

THE GENTLEMAN. I'm sorry, I haven't any change.

THE FLOWER GIRL. I can give you change, Captain,

THE GENTLEMEN. For a sovereign? I've nothing less.

THE FLOWER GIRL. Garn! Oh do buy a flower off me, Captain. I can change half-a-crown. Take this for tuppence.

THE GENTLEMAN. Now don't be troublesome: there's a good girl. [Trying his pockets] I really haven't any change—Stop: here's three hapence, if that's any use to you [he retreats to the other pillar].

THE FLOWER GIRL [disappointed, but thinking three halfpence better than nothing] Thank you, sir.

THE BYSTANDER [to the girl] You be careful: give him a flower for it. There's a bloke here behind taking down every blessed word you're saying. [All turn to the man who is taking notes].

THE FLOWER GIRL [springing up terrified] I ain't done nothing wrong by speaking to the gentleman. I've a right to sell flowers if I keep off the kerb. [Hysterically] I'm a respectable girl: so help me, I never spoke to him except to ask him to buy a flower off me. [General hubbub, mostly sympathetic to the flower girl, but deprecating her excessive sensibility. Cries of Don't start hollerin. Who's hurting you? Nobody's going to touch you. What's the good of fussing? Steady on. Easy, easy, etc., come from the elderly staid spectators, who pat her comfortingly. Less patient ones bid her shut her head, or ask her roughly what is wrong with her. A remoter group, not knowing what the matter is, crowd in and increase the noise with question and answer: What's the row? What she do? Where is he? A tec taking her down. What! him? Yes: him over there: Took money off the gentleman, etc. The flower girl, distraught and mobbed, breaks through them to the gentleman, crying mildly] Oh, sir, don't let him charge me. You dunno what it means to me. They'll take away my character and drive me on the streets for speaking to gentlemen. They—

THE NOTE TAKER [coming forward on her right, the rest crowding after him] There, there, there, there! Who's hurting you, you silly girl? What do you take me for?

THE BYSTANDER. It's all right: he's a gentleman: look at his boots. [Explaining to the note taker] She thought you was a copper's nark, sir.

THE NOTE TAKER [with quick interest] What's a copper's nark?

THE BYSTANDER [inept at definition] It's a—well, it's a copper's nark, as you might say. What else would you call it? A sort of informer.

THE FLOWER GIRL [still hysterical] I take my Bible oath I never said a word—

THE NOTE TAKER [overbearing but good-humored] Oh, shut up, shut up. Do I look like a policeman?

THE FLOWER GIRL [far from reassured] Then what did you take down my words for? How do I know whether you took me down right? You just show me what you've wrote about me. [The note taker opens his book and holds it steadily under her nose, though the pressure of the mob trying to read it over his shoulders would upset a weaker man]. What's that? That ain't proper writing. I can't read that.

THE NOTE TAKER. I can. [Reads, reproducing her pronunciation exactly]

"Cheer ap, Keptin; n' haw ya flahr orf a pore gel."

THE FLOWER GIRL [much distressed] It's because I called him Captain. I meant no harm. [To the gentleman] Oh, sir, don't let him lay a charge agen me for a word like that. You—

THE GENTLEMAN. Charge! I make no charge. [To the note taker] Really, sir, if you are a detective, you need not begin protecting me against molestation by young women until I ask you. Anybody could see that the girl meant no harm.

THE BYSTANDERS GENERALLY [demonstrating against police espionage] Course they could. What business is it of yours? You mind your own affairs. He wants promotion, he does. Taking down people's words! Girl never said a word to him. What harm if she did? Nice thing a girl can't shelter from the rain without being insulted, etc., etc., etc. [She is conducted by the more sympathetic demonstrators back to her plinth, where she resumes her seat and struggles with her emotion].

THE BYSTANDER. He ain't a tec. He's a blooming busybody: that's what he is. I tell you, look at his boots.

THE NOTE TAKER [turning on him genially] And how are all your people down at Selsey?

THE BYSTANDER [suspiciously] Who told you my people come from Selsey?

THE NOTE TAKER. Never you mind. They did. [To the girl] How do you come to be up so far east? You were born in Lisson Grove.

THE FLOWER GIRL [appalled] Oh, what harm is there in my leaving Lisson Grove? It wasn't fit for a pig to live in; and I had to pay four-and-six a week. [In tears] Oh, boo—hoo—oo—

THE NOTE TAKER. Live where you like; but stop that noise.

THE GENTLEMAN [to the girl] Come, come! he can't touch you: you have a right to live where you please.

A SARCASTIC BYSTANDER [thrusting himself between the note taker and the gentleman] Park Lane, for instance. I'd like to go into the Housing Question with you, I would.

THE FLOWER GIRL [subsiding into a brooding melancholy over her basket, and talking very low-spiritedly to herself] I'm a good girl, I am.

THE SARCASTIC BYSTANDER [not attending to her] Do you know where I come from?

THE NOTE TAKER [promptly] Hoxton.

Titterings. Popular interest in the note taker's performance increases.

THE SARCASTIC ONE [amazed] Well, who said I didn't? Bly me! You know everything, you do.

THE FLOWER GIRL [still nursing her sense of injury] Ain't no call to meddle with me, he ain't.

THE BYSTANDER [to her] Of course he ain't. Don't you stand it from him. [To the note taker] See here: what call have you to know about people what never offered to meddle with you? Where's your warrant?

SEVERAL BYSTANDERS [encouraged by this seeming point of law] Yes: where's your warrant?

THE FLOWER GIRL. Let him say what he likes. I don't want to have no truck with him.

THE BYSTANDER. You take us for dirt under your feet, don't you? Catch you taking liberties with a gentleman!

THE SARCASTIC BYSTANDER. Yes: tell HIM where he come from if you want to go fortune-telling.

THE NOTE TAKER. Cheltenham, Harrow, Cambridge, and India.

THE GENTLEMAN. Quite right. [Great laughter. Reaction in the note taker's favor. Exclamations of He knows all about it. Told him proper. Hear him tell the toff where he come from? etc.]. May I ask, sir, do you do this for your living at a music hall?

THE NOTE TAKER. I've thought of that. Perhaps I shall someday.

The rain has stopped; and the persons on the outside of the crowd begin to drop off.

THE FLOWER GIRL [resenting the reaction] He's no gentleman, he ain't, to interfere with a poor girl.

THE DAUGHTER [out of patience, pushing her way rudely to the front and displacing the gentleman, who politely retires to the other side of the pillar] What on earth is Freddy doing? I shall get pneumonia if I stay in this draught any longer.

THE NOTE TAKER [to himself, hastily making a note of her pronunciation of "monia"] Earlscourt.

THE DAUGHTER [violently] Will you please keep your impertinent remarks to yourself?

THE NOTE TAKER. Did I say that out loud? I didn't mean to. I beg your pardon. Your mother's Epsom, unmistakably.

THE MOTHER [advancing between her daughter and the note taker] How very curious! I was brought up in Largelady Park, near Epsom.

THE NOTE TAKER [uproariously amused] Ha! ha! What a devil of a name! Excuse me. [To the daughter] You want a cab, do you?

THE DAUGHTER. Don't dare speak to me.

THE MOTHER. Oh, please, please Clara. [Her daughter repudiates her with an angry shrug and retires haughtily.] We should be so grateful to you, sir, if you found us a cab. [The note taker produces a whistle]. Oh, thank you. [She joins her daughter]. The note taker blows a piercing blast.

THE SARCASTIC BYSTANDER. There! I knew he was a plain-clothes copper.

THE BYSTANDER. That ain't a police whistle: that's a sporting whistle.

THE FLOWER GIRL [still preoccupied with her wounded feelings] He's no right to take away my character. My character is the same to me as any lady's.

THE NOTE TAKER. I don't know whether you've noticed it; but the rain stopped about two minutes ago.

THE BYSTANDER. So it has. Why didn't you say so before? and us losing our time listening to your silliness. [He walks off towards the Strand].

THE SARCASTIC BYSTANDER. I can tell where you come from. You come from Anwell. Go back there.

THE NOTE TAKER [helpfully] Hanwell.

THE SARCASTIC BYSTANDER [affecting great distinction of speech] Thank you, teacher. Haw haw! So long [he touches his hat with mock respect and strolls off].

THE FLOWER GIRL. Frightening people like that! How would he like it himself.

THE MOTHER. It's quite fine now, Clara. We can walk to a motor bus. Come. [She gathers her skirts above her ankles and hurries off towards the Strand].

THE DAUGHTER. But the cab—[her mother is out of hearing]. Oh, how tiresome! [She follows angrily].

All the rest have gone except the note taker, the gentleman, and the flower girl, who sits arranging her basket, and still pitying herself in murmurs.

THE FLOWER GIRL. Poor girl! Hard enough for her to live without being worried and chivied.

THE GENTLEMAN [returning to his former place on the note taker's left] How do you do it, if I may ask?

THE NOTE TAKER. Simply phonetics. The science of speech. That's my profession; also my hobby. Happy is the man who can make a living by his hobby! You can spot an Irishman or a Yorkshireman by his brogue. I can place any man within six miles. I can place him within two miles in London. Sometimes within two streets.

THE FLOWER GIRL. Ought to be ashamed of himself, unmanly coward!

THE GENTLEMAN. But is there a living in that?

THE NOTE TAKER. Oh yes. Quite a fat one. This is an age of upstarts. Men begin in Kentish Town with 80 pounds a year, and end in Park Lane with a hundred thousand. They want to drop Kentish Town; but they give themselves away every time they open their mouths. Now I can teach them.

THE FLOWER GIRL. Let him mind his own business and leave a poor girl—

THE NOTE TAKER [explosively] Woman: cease this detestable boohooing instantly; or else seek the shelter of some other place of worship.

THE FLOWER GIRL [with feeble defiance] I've a right to be here if I like, same as you.

THE NOTE TAKER. A woman who utters such depressing and disgusting sounds has no right to be anywhere—no right to live. Remember that you are a human being with a soul and the divine gift of articulate speech: that your native language is the language of Shakespeare and Milton and The Bible; and don't sit there crooning like a bilious pigeon.

THE FLOWER GIRL [quite overwhelmed, and looking up at him in mingled wonder and deprecation without daring to raise her head] Ah—ah—ah—ow—ow—oo!

THE NOTE TAKER [whipping out his book] Heavens! what a sound! [He writes; then holds out the book and reads, reproducing her vowels exactly] Ah—ah—ah—ow—ow—ow—oo!

THE FLOWER GIRL [tickled by the performance, and laughing in spite of herself] Garn!

THE NOTE TAKER. You see this creature with her kerbstone English: the English that will keep her in the gutter to the end of her days. Well, sir, in three months I could pass that girl off as a duchess at an ambassador's garden party. I could even get her a place as lady's maid or shop assistant, which requires better English. That's the sort of thing I do for commercial millionaires. And on the profits of it I do genuine scientific work in phonetics, and a little as a poet on Miltonic lines.

Questions for discussion:

1. What social reality can we learn from this play? What is the playwright's purpose of alluding to Greek mythology in naming this play?

2. Can language really change the fate of those with a low social status? Analyze the dialogues in this except and discuss the social problems reflected.

3. Who is the real controller of the flower girl's fate?

3.5　Appreciation of Selected Readings

萧伯纳出生在爱尔兰都柏林一个没落的资产阶级家庭，二十多岁移居英国，卷入了当时正在兴起的社会革命运动，对于资本主义暴露出的各种弊病深有感触，所以在他的戏剧创作中，我们可以看到他对一系列社会问题的揭发和对资本家的谴责。《卖花女》（*Pigmalion*）与古希腊神话 Pigmalion 同名，作为一部社会讽刺剧，它极大地扩展了神话故事的意义。该剧以对话形式描写了希金森教授对身份低微的卖花女 Eliza 进行语音训练，说上层社会的"文雅"英语，并最终使她获得英国上流社会的认可和接纳的故事。在幽默的语言对话中，萧伯纳展示了剧中人物的性格，深刻抨击了英国的社会等级观念。"*A woman who utters such depressing and disgusting sounds has no right to be anywhere—no right to live. Remember that you are a human being with a soul and the divine gift of articulate speech: that your native language is the language of Shakespear and Milton and The Bible; and don't sit there crooning like a bilious pigeon.*" 剧作家抓住口音（accent）这一细节，揭露了其背后的英国社会阶级意识，包括出身、家世、教育、社会地位等。希金森教授抓住了口音，也就抓住了英国资本主义人士所稀罕的东西，通过语音训练这一"实验"成功地将一个卖花女变成了人们眼中的公爵夫人，嘲讽了整个贵族阶级。当然，萧伯纳的嘲讽也是双重的，一方面他嘲讽的是那些被模仿的上层阶级，另一方面他也揭露了那些鹦鹉学舌的小资产阶级的丑态。

　　皮格马利翁（Pigmalion）是古希腊神话中的塞浦路斯国王，他将自己的全部热情和挚爱倾注到自己雕刻的少女雕像上，少女像被他的痴情所动，变成了真人，并成为他的妻子。萧伯纳在此剧本中将语音学教授希金森比作皮格马利翁，自然让读者想到卖花女对应的就是 Galatea，但是剧本中的讽刺再一次出现：卖花女 Eliza 最终另嫁他人。她虽然出生于伦敦的平民窟，但是在向上流社会学习的过程中，她逐渐地成长为不同于上流社会的小姐们，而是一位完全有自己独立主见，斗争力旺盛的新型女性。

　　该戏剧借用希腊神话故事作为戏剧名字，如今皮格马利翁效应告诉我们，对一个人传递积极的期望，就会使他进步得更快，发展得更好。反之，向一个人传递消极的期望则会使人自暴自弃，放弃努力。该戏剧也使得这种积极思想得到普遍的认可。社会主义人生观是一种积极的价值观。当代青年大学生应该树立正确的世界观、人生观和价值观，以积极的心态面对学习和生活。

3.6　Supplementary Reading

The Story of Pygmalion

By Ovid

One man, Pygmalion, who had seen these women

Leading their shameful lives, shocked at the vices

Nature has given the female disposition

Only too often, chose to live alone,

To have no woman in his bed. But meanwhile

He made, with marvelous art, an ivory statue,

As white as snow, and gave it greater beauty

Than any girl could have, and fell in love

With his own workmanship. The image seemed

That of a virgin, truly, almost living,

And wiling, save that modesty prevented,

To take on movement. The best art, they say,

Is that which conceals art, and so Pygmalion

Marvels, and loves the body he has fashioned.

He would often move his hands to test and touch it,

Could this be flesh, or was it ivory only?

No, it could not be ivory. His kisses,

He fancies, she returns; he speaks to her,

Holds her, believes his fingers almost leave

An imprint on her limbs, and fears to bruise her.

He pays her compliments and brings her presents

Such as girls love, smooth pebbles, winding shells.

Little pet birds, flowers with a thousand colors,

Lilies, and painted balls, and lumps of amber.

He decks her limbs with dresses, and her fingers

Wear rings which he puts on, and he brings a necklace,

And earings, and a ribbon for her bosom,

And all of these become her, but she seems

Even more lovely naked, and he spreads

A crimson coverlet for her to lie on,

Takes her to bed, puts a soft pillow under

Her head, as if she felt it, calls her Darling,

My darling love!

'And Venus' holiday

Came round, and all the people of the island

Were holding festival, and snow-white heifers

Their horns al tipped with gold, stood at the alters,

Where incense burned, and, timidly, Pygmalion

Made offering, and prayed: 'If you can give

All things, O gods, I pray my wife may be

(He almost said, My ivory girl, but dared not)-

One like my ivory girl.' And golden Venus

Was there, and understood the prayer's intention,

And showed her presence, with the bright flame leaping

Thrice on the altar, and Pygmalion came

Back where the maiden lay, and lay beside her,

And kised her, and she semed to glow, and kised her,

And stroked her breast, and felt the ivory soften

Under his fingers, as wax grows soft in sunshine,

Made pliable by handling. And Pygmalion

Wonders, and douts, is dubious and happy,

Plays lover again, and over and over touches

The body with his hand. It is a body!

The veins throb under the thumb. And oh, Pygmalion

Is lavish in his prayer and praise to Venus,

No words are good enough. The lips he kisses

Are real indeed, the ivory girl can feel them,

And blushes and responds, and the eyes open

At once on lover and heaven, and Venus blesses

The mariage she has made. The crescent moon

Fills to ful orb, nine times, and wanes again,

And then adaughter is born, a girl named Paphos,

From whom the island later takes its name.

Unit 4   Theme in Drama: *The Glass Menagerie*

4.1   Elements of Drama: Theme

Theme refers to the central, deeper meaning of a written work. Writers typically will convey the theme to allow the readers or audience to perceive and interpret it. As readers infer, reflect, and analyze a literary theme, they develop a greater understanding of the work itself and can employ this understanding beyond the literary work as a means of grasping a better sense of the world. And theme is often what creates a memorable and significant experience of a literary work for the reader.

Themes are often open to the reader's perception and interpretation which means that there are a thousand Hamlets in a thousand people's eyes. Therefore, theme allows for literature to remain meaningful and "living" works that can be revisited and analyzed in perpetuity by many readers at once or by a single reader across time.

For example, William Shakespeare's well-known tragedy, *Romeo and Juliet*, has been performed and read countless times and by countless people since its publication in 1597:

Come, gentle night; come, loving, black-browed night;

Give me my Romeo; and, when I shall die,

Take him and cut him out in little stars,

And he will make the face of heaven so fine

That all the world will be in love with night.

Even those who have not directly heard or read the lines of this play are familiar with its theme, the power of romantic love and its potentially devastating effects.

Many works of literature share common themes and central ideas. Theme allows the author to present and reveal all aspects of human nature and the human condition, and the readers to enhance the enjoyment and significance of a literary work by encouraging different thoughts and interpretations.

4.2   Tennessee Williams and His Achievements

Tennessee Williams is widely considered the greatest Southern playwright and one of the greatest playwrights in the history of American drama. He was born Thomas Lanier Williams in Mississippi in 1911. The second of three children, his family life was full of tension. His mother valued refinement and good manners. His father, a traveling salesman, paid little attention to good breeding. In 1937 he attended the State University of Iowa to study playwriting. After graduation, Williams travelled around the United States and settled down in New Orleans, supporting himself by doing odd jobs. At the same time, he changed his name from "Tom" to "Tennessee" which was the state of his father's birth. Williams' first play, *Battle of Angels*, was a failure. In 1944, what many consider to be his best play, *The Glass Menagerie*, had a very successful run in Chicago and a year later burst its way onto Broadway. *The Glass Menagerie* won the New York Drama Critics' Circle Award for best play of the season. *A Streetcar Named Desire* in 1947 was his next important play. *Cat on a Hot Tin Roof*, another Pulitzer Prize-winning play, was produced in 1955.

Williams struggled with depression throughout most of his life and lived with the constant fear. Tennessee Williams met and fell in love with Frank Merlo in 1947, who was a steadying influence in Williams' chaotic life. But in 1961, Merlo died of Lung Cancer and the playwright went into a deep depression that lasted for ten years. During his last years, Williams continued writing, but one play after another failed. To ease his pain, he turned to drink and drugs and died on February 24, 1983.

4.3　The Plots of the Drama

The Glass Menagerie is written by a popular American writer, Tennessee Williams. It was premiered in Chicago in 1944 and became an instant hit: Its Broadway production ran for 561 performances bringing both fortune and popularity for the playwright and freeing him to write plays full-time. Set in St. Louis during the Great Depression when the United States was on the brink of World War II, this "memory play" draws heavily from the agonies of Williams's own family. Major themes include the difficulty of accepting reality, the impossibility of true escape and the unrelenting power of memory.

The playwright notes in the Production Notes of *The Glass Menagerie* that "nostalgia—is the first condition of the play". All the characters in the play are haunted by their memories, which prevent them from finding happiness in their present lives. It revolves around a mother, her shy and introverted daughter, Laura, and her artist son, Tom. Amanda is a single mother, whose husband had deserted the family years back in the past before the play begins.

The play starts with Tom Wingfield, Amanda Wingfield's son recalling his life. The setting is in the 1930's in a shabby apartment in St. Louis. Living in a middle-class apartment in St. Louis, his mother Amanda takes care of her crippled daughter and her working son, Tom. Amanda recalls her glory days when the boys used to chase her due to her beautiful looks and outgoing personality. Tom is extremely unhappy with his present life. Despite seemingly being a budding poet, Tom Wingfield does not find enough time due to his constant worry of everyday preoccupations and penchant for movies that he watches all night. This future worry and not-so-bright prospectus of her son Tom, who is working in a warehouse, has become constant worry for her. She constantly nags Tom about ways to improve himself, which only increases his irritation and desire to escape from home.

Tom's sister, Laura, is slightly handicapped and too shy to interact with people outside her family. She lives largely in the dream world of her collection of artificial glass animals and old phonograph records. Now her main anxiety is her daughter. Laura does not seem to win any gentleman's attention. Looking at her daughter's youth, Amanda becomes obsessed with the idea of finding a gentleman for her. At dinner Amanda tells her daughter, Laura, to stay polite and pretty for her gentlemen callers even though she never had any callers and never expected one.

Amanda believes that marrying Laura off is the only option for her. She, therefore, asks Tom to bring home someone from his workplace to meet his sister. A few days later Amanda comes home from Laura's school after finding out that Laura had dropped out several months earlier. Amanda is shocked and wonders what they will do with their lives since Laura refuses to try to help and spends all her time playing with her glass menagerie and her old phonograph records. Amanda decides that they must have a gentleman caller for Laura, and Laura tells her that she has liked only one boy in her whole life, a high school boy named Jim.

When Tom goes out to the movies that night, Amanda scolds him and asks him to do something useful rather than going to the movies every night. They have an argument, and the next morning after Tom apologizes, Amanda asks him to find some nice gentleman caller for Laura and to bring him home for dinner.

A few days later, Tom brings home his workmate, a young man, Jim O'Connor. When Amanda comes to know about the arrival of Jim, she becomes jubilant, seeing the prospects of meeting with the future of her daughter. When Jim comes, she starts recalling her own budding youthful period and her own looks. It turns out that Laura knew Jim and she had a crush in high school. He seems like Laura's rescuer. As Jim and Laura talk, she loses some of her shyness and becomes rather charming. Jim teaches Laura to dance, and even kisses her. While dancing, Jim breaks the horn off Laura's glass unicorn, symbolically releasing her from her dream world. Unfortunately, Jim is engaged. Later after having kissed her, Jim must explain that he is already engaged. Amanda, upon learning this, refuses to hear Tom's explanation of his ignorance about such a thing and lashes out at him for cheating her. Tom picked up and left the house, asking his sister to extinguish the candles.

The play ends on a sad note of Tom thinking back on his sister Laura whom he can never forget. The play ends with Tom some years in the future.

4.4 Selected Readings

The Glass Menagerie

(Excerpts)

Scene IV

[The interior is dark. Faint light in the alley.

A deep-voiced bell in a church is tolling the hour of five as the scene commences.

TOM appears at the top of the alley. After each solemn boom of the bell in the tower, he shakes a little noise-maker or rattle as if to express the tiny spasm of man in contrast to the sustained power and dignity of the Almighty. This and the unsteadiness of his advance make it evident that he has been drinking.

As he climbs the few steps to the fire-escape landing light steals up inside. LAURA appears in night-dress, observing TOM's empty bed in the front room.

TOM fishes in his pockets for door-key, removing a motley assortment of articles in the search, including a perfect shower of movie-ticket stubs and an empty bottle. At last he finds the key, but just as he is about to insert it, it slips from his fingers. He strikes a match and crouches below the door.]

Tom [bitterly]: One crack — and it falls through!

[LAURA opens the door.]

Laura: Tom! Tom, what are you doing?

Tom: Looking for a door-key.

Laura: Where have you been all this time?

Tom: I have been to the movies.

Laura: All this time at the movies?

Tom: There was a very long program. There was a Garbo picture and a Mickey Mouse and a travelogue and a newsreel and a preview of coming attractions. And there was an organ solo and a collection for the milk-fund — simultaneously — which ended up in a terrible fight between a fat lady and an usher!

Laura [innocently]: Did you have to stay through everything?

Tom: Of course! And, oh, I forgot! There was a big stage show! The headliner on this stage show was Malvolio the Magician. He performed wonderful tricks, many of them, such as pouring water back and forth between pitchers. First it turned to wine and then it turned to beer and then it turned to whisky. I knew it was whisky it finally turned into because he needed somebody to come up out of the audience to help him, and I came up—both shows! It was Kentucky Straight Bourbon. A very generous fellow, he gave souvenirs. [He pulls from his back pocket a shimmering rainbow-coloured scarf.] He gave me this. This is his magic scarf. You can have it, Laura. You wave it over a canary cage and you get a bowl of gold-fish. You wave it over the gold-fish bowl and they fly away canaries... But the wonderfullest trick of all was the coffin trick. We nailed him into a coffin and he got out of the coffin without removing one nail. [He has come inside.] There is a trick that would come in handy for me — get me out of this 2 by 4 situation! [Flops on to a bed and starts removing shoes.]

Laura: Tom — Shhh!

Tom: What're you shushing me for?

Laura: You'll wake up mother.

Tom: Goody, goody! Payer back for all those "Rise and Shines". [Lies down, groaning.] You know it don't take much intelligence to get yourself into a nailed-up coffin, Laura. But who in hell ever got himself out of one without removing one nail?

[As if in answer, the father's grinning photograph lights up.]

SCENE DIMS OUT

[Immediately following: The church bell is heard striking six. At the sixth stroke the alarm clock goes off in AMANDA's room, and after a few moments we hear her calling 'Rise and Shine! Rise and Shine! Laura, go tell your brother to rise and shine!']

Tom [sitting up slowly]: I'll rise—but I won't shine.

[The light increases.]

Amanda: Laura, tell your brother his coffee is ready.

[LAURA slips into front room.]

Laura: Tom! It's nearly seven. Don't make mother nervous. [He stares at her stupidly. Beseechingly.] Tom, speak to mother this morning. Make up with her, apologize, speak to her!

Tom: She won't to me. It's her that started not speaking.

Laura: If you just say you're sorry she'll start speaking.

Tom: Her not speaking — is that such a tragedy?

Laura: Please — please!

Amanda [calling from kitchenette]: Laura, are you going to do what I asked you to do, or do I have to get dressed and go out myself?

Laura Going, going—soon as I get on my coat! [She pulls on a shapeless felt hat with nervous, jerky movement, pleadingly glancing at TOM. Rushes awkwardly for coat. The coat is one of AMANDA's, inaccurately made-over, the sleeves too short for LAURA.] But-ter and what else?

Amanda [entering upstage]: Just butter. Tell them to charge it.

Laura: Mother, they make such faces when I do that.

Amanda: Sticks and stones can break our bones, but the expression on Mr Garfinkel's face won't harm us! Tell your brother his coffee is getting cold.

Laura [at door]: Do what I asked you, will you, will you, Tom?

[He looks sullenly away.]

Amanda: Laura, go now or just don't go at all!

Laura [rushing out]: Going — going! [A second later she cries out. TOM springs up and crosses to door. AMANDA rushes anxiously in. TOM opens the door.]

Tom: Laura?

Laura: I'm all right. I slipped, but I'm all right.

Amanda [peering anxiously after her]: If anyone breaks a leg on those fire-escape steps, the landlord ought to be sued for every cent he possesses! [She shuts door. Remembers she isn't speaking and returns to other room.]

[As TOM enters listlessly for his coffee, she turns her back to him and stands rigidly facing the window on the gloomy grey vault of the areaway. Its light on her face with its aged but childish features is cruelly sharp, satirical as a Daumier print.

MUSIC UNDER: 'AVE MARIE'.

TOM glances sheepishly but sullenly at her averted figure and slumps at the table. The coffee is scalding hot; he sips it and gasps and spits it back in the cup. At his gasp, AMANDA catches her breath and half turns. Then catches herself and turns back to window.

TOM blows on his coffee, glancing sidewise at his mother. She clears her throat. TOM clears his. He starts to rise. Sinks back down again, scratches his head, clears his throat again. AMANDA coughs. TOM raises his cup in both hands to blow on it, his eyes staring over the rim of it at his mother for several moments. Then he slowly sets the cup down and awkwardly and hesitantly rises from the chair.]

Tom [hoarsely]: Mother. I — I apologize, Mother. [AMANDA draws a quick, shuddering breath. Her face works grotesquely. She breaks into childlike tears.] I'm sorry for what I said, for everything that I said; I didn't mean it.

Amanda [sobbingly]: My devotion has made me a witch and so I make myself hateful to my children!

Tom: No, you don't.

Amanda: I worry so much, don't sleep, it makes me nervous!

Tom [gently]: I understand that.

Amanda: I've had to put up a solitary battle all these years. But you're my right-hand bower! Don't fall down, don't fall!

Tom [gently]: I try, Mother.

Amanda [with great enthusiasm]: Try and you will SUCCEED! [The notion makes her breathless.] Why, you—you're just full of natural endowments! Both of my children — they're unusual children! Don't you think I know it? I'm so—proud! Happy and—feel I've — so much to be thankful for but— Promise me one thing. Son!

Tom: What, Mother?

Amanda: Promise, Son, you'll — never be a drunkard!

Tom [turns to her grinning]: I will never be a drunkard, Mother.

Amanda: That's what frightened me so, that you'd be drinking! Eat a bowl of Purina!

Tom: Just coffee, Mother.

Amanda: Shredded wheat biscuit?

Tom: No. No, Mother, just coffee.

Amanda: You can't put in a day's work on an empty stomach. You've gotten minutes — don't gulp! Drinking too-hot liquids makes cancer of the stomach... Put cream in.

Tom: No, thank you.

Amanda: To cool it.

Tom: No! No, thank you, I want it black.

Amanda: I know, but it's not good for you. We have to do all that we can to build our-selves up. In these trying times we live in, all that we have to cling to is—each other.... That's why it's so important to—Tom, I —I sent out your sister so I could discuss something with you. If you hadn't spoken, I would have spoken to you. [Sits down.]

Tom [gently]: What is it, Mother, that you want to discuss?

Amanda: Laura!

[TOM puts his cup down slowly.

LEGEND ON SCREEN: "LAURA".

MUSIC: "THE GLASS MENAGERIE".]

Tom: —Oh. —Laura...

Amanda [touching his sleeve]: You know how Laura is. So quiet but—still water runs deep! She notices things and I think she-broods about them. [TOM looks up.] A few days ago I came in and she was crying.

Tom: What about?

Amanda: You.

Tom: Me?

Amanda: She has an idea that you're not happy here.

Tom: What gave her that idea?

Amanda: What gives her any idea? However, you do act strangely. I'm not criticizing, understand that! I know your ambitions do not lie in the warehouse, that like everybody in the whole wide world—you've had to—make sacrifices, but—Tom—Tom—life's not easy, it calls for—Spartan endurance! There's so many things in my heart that I cannot describe to you! I've never told you but I loved your father....

Tom [gently]: I know that, Mother.

Amanda: And you—when I see you taking after his ways! Staying out late—and—well, you had been drinking the night you were in that—terrifying condition! Laura says that you hate the apartment and that you go out nights to get away from it! Is that true, Tom?

Tom: No. You say there's so much in your heart that you can't describe to me. That's true of me, too. There's so much in my heart that I can't describe to you! So let's respect each other's—

Amanda: But, why—why, Tom —are you always so restless? Where do you go to, nights?

Tom: I—go to the movies.

Amanda: Why do you go to the movies so much, Tom?

Tom: I go to the movies because—I like adventure. Adventure is something I don't have much of at work, so I go to the movies.

Amanda: But, Tom, you go to the movies entirely too much!

Tom: I like a lot of adventure.

[AMANDA looks baffled, then hurt. As the familiar inquisition resumes he becomes hard and impatient again. AMANDA slips back into her querulous attitude towards him.

IMAGE ON SCREEN: SAILING VESSEL WITH JOLLY ROGER.]

Amanda: Most young men find adventure in their careers.

Tom: Then most young men are not employed in a warehouse.

Amanda: The world is full of young men employed in warehouses and offices and factories.

Tom: Do all of them find adventure in their careers?

Amanda: They do or they do without it! Not everybody has a craze for adventure.

Tom: Man is by instinct a lover, a hunter, a fighter, and none of those instincts are given much play at the warehouse!

Amanda: Man is by instinct! Don't quote instinct to me! Instinct is something that people have got away from! It belongs to animals! Christian adults don't want it!

Tom: What do Christian adults want, then, Mother?

Amanda: Superior things! Things of the mind and the spirit! Only animals have to satisfy instincts! Surely your aims are somewhat higher than theirs! Than monkeys—pigs—

Tom: I reckon they're not.

Amanda: You're joking. However, that isn't what I wanted to discuss.

Tom [rising]: I haven't much time.

Amanda [pushing his shoulders]: Sit down.

Tom: You want me to punch in red at the warehouse, Mother?

Amanda: You have five minutes. I want to talk about Laura.

[LEGEND: "PLANS AND PROVISIONS".]

Tom: All right! What about Laura?

Amanda: We have to be making some plans and provisions for her. She's older than you, two years, and nothing has happened. She just drifts along doing nothing. It frightens me terribly how she just drifts along.

Tom: I guess she's the type that people call home girls.

Amanda: There's no such type, and if there is, it's a pity! That is unless the home is hers, with a husband!

Tom: What?

Amanda: Oh, I can see the handwriting on the wall as plain as I see the nose in front of my face! It's terrifying! More and more you remind me of your father! He was out all hours without explanation! Then left! Good-bye! And me with the bag to hold. I saw that letter you got from the Merchant Marine. I know what you're dreaming of. I'm not standing here blindfolded.

Very well, then. Then do it! But not till there's somebody to take your place.

Tom: What do you mean?

Amanda: I mean that as soon as Laura has got somebody to take care of her, married, a home of her own, independent — why, then you'll be free to go wherever you please, on land, on sea, whichever way the wind blows you!

But until that time you've got to look out for your sister. I don't say me because I'm old and don't matter! I say for your sister because she's young and dependent.

I put her in business college— a dismal failure! Frightened her so it made her sick at the stomach.

I took her over to the Young People's League at the church. Another fiasco. She spoke to nobody, nobody spoke to her. Now all she does is fool with those pieces of glass and play those worn-out records. What kind of a life is that for a girl to lead?

Tom: What can I do about it?

Amanda: Overcome selfishness!

Self, self, self is all that you ever think of!

[TOM springs up and crosses to get his coat. It is ugly and bulky. He pulls on a cap with earmuffs.]

Where is your muffler? Put your wool muffler on! [He snatches it angrily from the closet and tosses it around his neck and pulls both ends tight.] Tom! I haven't said what I had in mind to ask you.

Tom: I'm too late to —

Amanda [catching his arm — very importunately. Then shyly]: Down at the warehouse, aren't there some —nice young men?

Tom: No!

Amanda: There must be—some…

Tom: Mother—

[Gesture.]

Amanda: Find out one that's clean-living — doesn't drink and — ask him out for sister!

Tom: What?

Amanda: For sister! To meet! Get acquainted!

Tom [stamping to door]: Oh, my go—osh!

Amanda: Will you? [He opens door. Imploringly.] Will you? [He starts down.] Will you? Will you, dear?

Tom [calling back]: YES!

[AMANDA closes the door hesitantly and with a troubled but faintly hopeful expression.

SCREEN IMAGE: GLAMOUR MAGAZINE COVER. Spot AMANDA at phone.]

Amanda: Ella Cartwright? This is Amanda Winglield! How are you, honey? How is that kidney condition? [Count five.] Horrors! [Count five.] You're a Christian martyr, yes, honey, that's what you are, a Christian martyr! Well, I just now happened to notice in my little red book that your subscription to the Companion has just run out! I knew that you wouldn't want to miss out on the wonderful serial starting in this issue. It's by Bessie Mae Hopper, the first thing she's written since Honeymoon for three. Wasn't that a strange and interesting story? Well, this one is even lovelier, I believe. It has a sophisticated, society background. It's all about the horsey set on Long Island!

Questions for discussion:

1.   Why is the play entitled "The Glass Menagerie" ? In what way can the glass menagerie be an effective symbol in signifying the theme of the play? How can we interpret Laura's unicorn?

2. How to understand the conflict between Tom's conception of the poet's role and his feeling of obligation to his family. Is he justified in abandoning his family at the end of the play? Is Tom's escape as complete as his father's?

3. In his address to the audience that begins the play, Tom says that Jim "is the most realistic character in the play ... as emissary of reality that we were somehow set apart from." What is the world of reality Jim representing? What sort of person is Jim O'Connor? How do you compare him with Tom and Laura?

4. Who is the central character in the play? Why?

4.5 Appreciation of Selected Readings

田纳西·威廉姆斯是第二次世界大战后最杰出的美国剧作家之一，他一生创作了约 35 部戏剧。美国 19 世纪 30 年代经历的经济大萧条使社会经济遭受重创，给每一个圣·路易斯普通家庭的普通人生活带来了重大影响。该戏剧作品正是通过书写这样的家庭来刻画没落的美国南方人，他们是"受害者、逃避者、残废者、与环境格格不入者和寂寞者"。如同剧中人，他们生活在回忆美好过往之中，却又如同剧中女儿劳拉的玻璃制品那样虽透明晶莹、小巧玲珑却容易破碎。在剧本的末尾处，儿子汤姆告诉观众他不久就会步父亲的后尘，离家而去，浪迹天涯。而母亲吹灭象征着一线希望的烛火，暗示了人们将继续生活在"永恒黑暗"之中，无处可逃的悲惨现实。和同时代的其他南方文学作家，特别是小说家一样，田纳西·威廉姆斯所关注的是"在一个没有传统、没有价值的社会中处于孤寂状态的个人"（刘海平，卷四，2002：65）。对个体命运的关注成就了这位 20 世纪的伟大剧作家。

在社会变革之际，青年的作用是巨大的。五四运动以来，无数中国青年为了民族独立与国家富强义无反顾，前仆后继。作为新时代的中国大学生，作为国家培养出来的当代青年，面对困难时，要牢记使命，勇敢接受生活中的各种挑战，应当树立远大的志向，肩负起建设繁荣、富强的社会主义国家的责任与担当，而不是像剧中人那样逃避现实。

4.6   Supplementary Reading

The Way of the World

by William Congreve

ACT I.

SCENE I.

A Chocolate-house.

MIRABELL and FAINALL rising from cards. BETTY waiting.

MIRA: You are a fortunate man, Mr. Fainall.

FAIN: Have we done?

MIRA: What you please. I'll play on to entertain you.

FAIN: No, I'll give you your revenge another time, when you are not so indifferent; you are thinking of something else now, and play too negligently: the coldness of a losing gamester lessens the pleasure of the winner. I'd no more play with a man that slighted his ill fortune than I'd make love to a woman who undervalued the loss of her reputation.

MIRA: You have a taste extremely delicate, and are for refining on your pleasures.

FAIN: Prithee, why so reserved? Something has put you out of humour.

MIRA: Not at all: I happen to be grave to-day, and you are gay; that's all.

FAIN: Confess, Millamant and you quarrelled last night, after I left you; my fair cousin has some humours that would tempt the patience of a Stoic. What, some coxcomb came in, and was well received by her, while you were by?

MIRA: Witwoud and Petulant, and what was worse, her aunt, your wife's mother, my evil genius—or to sum up all in her own name, my old Lady Wishfort came in.

FAIN: Oh, there it is then: she has a lasting passion for you, and with reason.—What, then my wife was there?

MIRA: Yes, and Mrs. Marwood and three or four more, whom I never saw before; seeing me, they all put on their grave faces, whispered one another, then complained aloud of the vapours, and after fell into a profound silence.

FAIN: They had a mind to be rid of you.

MIRA: For which reason I resolved not to stir. At last the good old lady broke through her painful taciturnity with an invective against long visits. I would not have understood her, but Millamant joining in the argument, I rose and with a constrained smile told her, I thought nothing was so easy as to know when a visit began to be troublesome; she reddened and I withdrew, without expecting her reply.

FAIN: You were to blame to resent what she spoke only in compliance with her aunt.

MIRA: She is more mistress of herself than to be under the necessity of such a resignation.

FAIN: What? Though half her fortune depends upon her marrying with my lady's approbation?

MIRA: I was then in such a humour, that I should have been better pleased if she had been less discreet.

FAIN: Now I remember, I wonder not they were weary of you; last night was one of their cabal-nights: they have 'em three times a week and meet by turns at one another's apartments, where they come together like the coroner's inquest, to sit upon the murdered reputations of the week. You and I are excluded, and it was once proposed that all the male sex should be excepted; but somebody moved that to avoid scandal there might be one man of the community, upon which motion Witwoud and Petulant were enrolled members.

MIRA: And who may have been the foundress of this sect? My Lady Wishfort, I warrant, who publishes her detestation of mankind, and full of the vigour of fifty-five, declares for a friend and ratafia; and let posterity shift for itself, she'll breed no more.

FAIN: The discovery of your sham addresses to her, to conceal your love to her niece, has provoked this separation. Had you dissembled better, things might have continued in the state of nature.

MIRA: I did as much as man could, with any reasonable conscience; I proceeded to the very last act of flattery with her, and was guilty of a song in her commendation. Nay, I got a friend to put her into a lampoon, and compliment her with the imputation of an affair with a young fellow, which I carried so far, that I told her the malicious town took notice that she was grown fat of a sudden; and when she lay in of a dropsy, persuaded her she was reported to be in labour.

The devil's in't, if an old woman is to be flattered further, unless a man should endeavour downright personally to debauch her: and that my virtue forbade me. But for the discovery of this amour, I am indebted to your friend, or your wife's friend, Mrs. Marwood.

FAIN: What should provoke her to be your enemy, unless she has made you advances which you have slighted? Women do not easily forgive omissions of that nature.

MIRA: She was always civil to me, till of late. I confess I am not one of those coxcombs who are apt to interpret a woman's good manners to her prejudice, and think that she who does not refuse 'em everything can refuse 'em nothing.

FAIN: You are a gallant man, Mirabell; and though you may have cruelty enough not to satisfy a lady's longing, you have too much generosity not to be tender of her honour. Yet you speak with an indifference which seems to be affected, and confesses you are conscious of a negligence.

MIRA: You pursue the argument with a distrust that seems to be unaffected, and confesses you are conscious of a concern for which the lady is more indebted to you than is your wife.

FAIN: Fie, fie, friend, if you grow censorious I must leave you:—I'll look upon the gamesters in the next room.

MIRA: Who are they?

FAIN: Petulant and Witwoud.—Bring me some chocolate.

MIRA: Betty, what says your clock?

BET: Turned of the last canonical hour, sir.

MIRA: How pertinently the jade answers me! Ha! almost one a' clock! [Looking on his watch.] Oh, y'are come!

SCENE II.

MIRABELL and FOOTMAN.

MIRA: Well, is the grand affair over? You have been something tedious.

SERV: Sir, there's such coupling at Pancras that they stand behind one another, as 'twere in a country-dance. Ours was the last couple to lead up; and no hopes appearing of dispatch, besides, the parson growing hoarse, we were afraid his lungs would have failed before it came to our turn; so we drove round to Duke's Place, and there they were riveted in a trice.

MIRA: So, so; you are sure they are married?

SERV: Married and bedded, sir; I am witness.

MIRA: Have you the certificate?

SERV: Here it is, sir.

MIRA: Has the tailor brought Waitwell's clothes home, and the new liveries?

SERV: Yes, sir.

MIRA: That's well. Do you go home again, d'ye hear, and adjourn the consummation till farther order; bid Waitwell shake his ears, and Dame Partlet rustle up her feathers, and meet me at one a' clock by Rosamond's pond, that I may see her before she returns to her lady. And, as you tender your ears, be secret.

SCENE III.

MIRABELL, FAINALL, BETTY.

FAIN: Joy of your success, Mirabell; you look pleased.

MIRA: Ay; I have been engaged in a matter of some sort of mirth, which is not yet ripe for discovery. I am glad this is not a cabal-night. I wonder, Fainall, that you who are married, and of consequence should be discreet, will suffer your wife to be of such a party.

FAIN: Faith, I am not jealous. Besides, most who are engaged are women and relations; and for the men, they are of a kind too contemptible to give scandal.

MIRA: I am of another opinion: the greater the coxcomb, always the more the scandal; for a woman who is not a fool can have but one reason for associating with a man who is one.

FAIN: Are you jealous as often as you see Witwoud entertained by Millamant?

MIRA: Of her understanding I am, if not of her person.

FAIN: You do her wrong; for, to give her her due, she has wit.

MIRA: She has beauty enough to make any man think so, and complaisance enough not to contradict him who shall tell her so.

FAIN: For a passionate lover methinks you are a man somewhat too discerning in the failings of your mistress.

MIRA: And for a discerning man somewhat too passionate a lover, for I like her with all her faults; nay, like her for her faults. Her follies are so natural, or so artful, that they become her, and those affectations which in another woman would be odious serve but to make her more agreeable. I'll tell thee, Fainall, she once used me with that insolence that in revenge I took her to pieces, sifted her, and separated her failings: I studied 'em and got 'em by rote. The catalogue was so large that I was not without hopes, one day or other, to hate her heartily. To which end I so used myself to think of 'em, that at length, contrary to my design and expectation, they gave me every hour less and less disturbance, till in a few days it became habitual to me to remember 'em without being displeased. They are now grown as familiar to me as my own frailties, and in all probability in a little time longer I shall like 'em as well.

FAIN: Marry her, marry her; be half as well acquainted with her charms as you are with her defects, and, my life on't, you are your own man again.

MIRA: Say you so?

FAIN: Ay, ay; I have experience. I have a wife, and so forth.

    SCENE IV.

    [To them] MESSENGER.

MESS: Is one Squire Witwoud here?

BET: Yes; what's your business?

MESS: I have a letter for him, from his brother Sir Wilfull, which I am charged to deliver into his own hands.

BET: He's in the next room, friend. That way.

    SCENE V.

    MIRABELL, FAINALL, BETTY.

MIRA: What, is the chief of that noble family in town, Sir Wilfull Witwoud?

FAIN: He is expected to-day. Do you know him?

MIRA: I have seen him; he promises to be an extraordinary person. I think you have the honour to be related to him.

FAIN: Yes; he is half-brother to this Witwoud by a former wife, who was sister to my Lady Wishfort, my wife's mother. If you marry Millamant, you must call cousins too.

MIRA: I had rather be his relation than his acquaintance.

FAIN: He comes to town in order to equip himself for travel.

MIRA: For travel! Why the man that I mean is above forty.

FAIN: No matter for that; 'tis for the honour of England that all Europe should know we have blockheads of all ages.

MIRA: I wonder there is not an act of parliament to save the credit of the nation and prohibit the exportation of fools.

FAIN: By no means, 'tis better as 'tis; 'tis better to trade with a little loss, than to be quite eaten up with being overstocked.

MIRA: Pray, are the follies of this knight-errant and those of the squire, his brother, anything related?

FAIN: Not at all: Witwoud grows by the knight like a medlar grafted on a crab. One will melt in your mouth and t'other set your teeth on edge; one is all pulp and the other all core.

MIRA: So one will be rotten before he be ripe, and the other will be rotten without ever being ripe at all.

FAIN: Sir Wilfull is an odd mixture of bashfulness and obstinacy. But when he's drunk, he's as loving as the monster in The Tempest, and much after the same manner. To give bother his due, he has something of good-nature, and does not always want wit.

MIRA: Not always: but as often as his memory fails him and his commonplace of comparisons. He is a fool with a good memory and some few scraps of other folks' wit. He is one whose conversation can never be approved, yet it is now and then to be endured. He has indeed one good quality: he is not exceptious, for he so passionately affects the reputation of understanding raillery that he will construe an affront into a jest, and call downright rudeness and ill language satire and fire.

FAIN: If you have a mind to finish his picture, you have an opportunity to do it at full length. Behold the original.

References

[1] Aristotle. Poetics[M]. New York: Dover, 1997.

[2] Aristotle. Hazard Adams. Ed. "Poetics," Critical Theory Since Plato [M]. San Diego: HBJ, 1971: 48-66.

[3] Bradley, Sculley & Harold W. Blodgett. Walt Whitman: Leaves of Grass [M]. New York: Norton, 1973.

[4] Brooks, Cleanth & Robert Penn Warren. Understanding Fiction [M]. London: Longman Publishing Group, 1988.

[5] Brooks, Peter. Reading for the Plot [M]. Boston: Harvard University Press, 1988.

[6] Chase, Richard, ed., Melville. A Collection of Critical Essays[A]. New Jersey: Englewood Cliffs, 1962.

[7] Foster, E. M.. Aspects of the Novel [M]. Boston: Houghton Mifflin Harcourt. 1970.

[8] Maugham, W. S., The Moon and Six Pence (e-book) [M]. New York: The Modern Library Library-New York, Random House,1919.

[9] Melville, Herman, Charles Child Walcult ed. Moby Dick, or THE WHALE [M]. New York: Bantam Classics, 2003.

[10] Selden, R.. A Reader's Guide to Contemporary Literary Theory [M]. Beijing: Foreign Language Teaching and Research Press, 2004.

[11] Shakespeare, William. The Complete Works of William Shakespeare [M]. London: Ramboro, 1993.

[12] Shaw, Bernard. Pygmalion: And Related Readings[M]. Boston: McDougal Littell, 1996.

[13] Walker, Alice. In Love & Trouble: Stories of Black Women [M]. New York: Open Road Integrated Media, 1973.

[14] Williams, Tennessee. The Glass Menagerie [M]. New York: Signet, 1987.

[15] 艾布拉姆斯. 文学术语汇编（A Glossary of Literary Terms）[M]. 7 版. 北京：

外语教学与研究出版社，2004.

[16] 常耀信. 美国文学简史[M]. 3 版. 天津：南开大学出版社，2008.

[17] 陈嘉. 英国文学史[M]. 北京：商务印书馆，1986.

[18] 胡家峦. 英国诗歌详注[M]. 北京：外语教学与研究出版社，2018.

[19] 霍松林. 古代文论名篇详注[M]. 上海：上海古籍出版社，2002.

[20] 蒋洪新. 英美诗歌选读[M]. 长沙：湖南师范大学出版社，2004.

[21] 李正栓. 白凤欣. 英语诗歌教程[M]. 北京：高等教育出版社，2008.

[22] 刘炳善. 英国文学简史（新增订本）[M]. 郑州：河南人民出版社，2007.

[23] 刘洊波. 文学导论[M]. 北京：高等教育出版社，2009.

[24] 刘海平，王守仁. 新编美国文学史（第四卷）[M]. 上海：上海外语教育出版社，2002.

[25] 刘守兰. 英美名诗解读[M]. 上海：上海外语教育出版社，2003.

[26] 邵锦娣. 白劲鹏. 文学导论[M]. 上海：上海外语教育出版社，2003.

[27] 王守仁. 英国文学选读[M]. 4 版. 北京：高等教育出版社，2014.

[28] 王佐良，等. 英国文学名篇选注（*An Anthology of English Literature Annotated in Chinese*）[M]. 北京：商务印书馆，2006.

[29] 习近平. 习近平谈治国理政（第二卷）[M]. 北京：外文出版社，2017.

[30] 虞建华. 英语短篇小说教程[M]. 2 版. 北京：高等教育出版社，2019.

[31] 曾艳钰.《英语专业本科教学指南》解读[J]. 外语界，2019.

[32] 中华人民共和国教育部. 教育部关于印发《高等学校课程思政建设指导纲要》[N]，2020.

[33] 朱望. 现代英国文学大家[M]. 北京：北京大学出版社，2011.

[34] Brief introduction about Joseph Conrad and his Literary works. [EB/OL]. [2022-07-19]. http://www.encycopedia.com/topic/Joseph_Conrad.aspx.

[35] The Project Gutenberg eBook of Moby-Dick; or The Whale, by Herman Melville [EB/OL]. [2022-08-23] https://www.gutenberg.org/files/2701/2701-h/2701-h.htm#link2HCH0116.

[36] William Shakespeare: The Complete Works by Linda Archin [EB/OL]. (2018-02-14) [2022-08-21]. https://www.william-shakespeare.info/act1-script-text-king-lear.htm.

[37] Tennessee Williams. [EB/OL]. [2022-09-14]. http://www.gatewayno.com/culture/TWilliams.html.

[38] George Bernard Shaw. [EB/OL]. (2019-10-12) [2022-10-15]. https://www.famous authors.org/george-bernard-shaw.

[39] Literary Devices. Definition and Examples of Literary Terms: Conflict Definition [EB/OL]. [2022-10-15]. https://literarydevices.net/conflict/.

[40] The Five Act Play (Dramatic Structure). Lesson Plans by Rebecca Ray [EB/OL]. [2022-12-09]. https://www.storyboardthat.com/articles/e/five-act-structure.